READY STEADY COOK 3

READY STEADY COOK 3

KEVIN WOODFORD

LESLEY WATERS

PHOTOGRAPHS BY
JULIET PIDDINGTON

BBC BOOKS

This book is published to accompany the television series *Ready Steady Cook*
which was first broadcast in Autumn 1994.
The series was produced by Bazal Productions.

Published by BBC Books, an imprint of BBC Worldwide Publishing,
BBC Worldwide Ltd, Woodlands, 80 Wood Lane, London W12 0TT.

First published 1997
Format © Bazal Productions
Recipes © Kevin Woodford and Lesley Waters
The moral right of the authors has been asserted
Photographs: Juliet Piddington
Home Economist: Sarah Ramsbottom
ISBN 0 563 38324 0

Set in Futura
Designed by Louise Morley
Printed by Martins the Printers Ltd, Berwick-upon-Tweed
Bound by Hunter & Foulis Ltd, Edinburgh
Colour separation by Radstock Reproductions Ltd, Midsomer Norton
Colour printing by Lawrence Allen Ltd, Weston-super-Mare
Cover printed by Belmont Press, Northampton

CONTENTS

INTRODUCTION

People are always asking me if the chefs on **Ready Steady Cook** actually know in advance what's in those mystery bags. I can honestly answer no, they are a complete surprise. The contestants choose their combination of foods carefully and our talented chefs really do have to create a culinary masterpiece on the spot within the all-important 20-minute time limit.

We know you like to try the delicious recipes you see on the screen. So, to save you scribbling away in front of the telly, we have put together another selection of some of our favourite dishes from the show. We've also put in plenty of those handy hints that can turn just another routine weekday supper into a gourmet feast.

Now all you have to do is pick a recipe, raid your larder and prepare yourself to **Ready Steady Cook**!

Fern Britton

x

Presenter, **Ready Steady Cook**

A Note on Ingredients and Techniques

Good-quality ingredients make all the difference to the taste of the finished dish. For best results, choose unsalted butter and extra virgin olive oil. Buy ripe, flavoursome tomatoes, and whenever possible, really fresh herbs. If a recipe specifies dried herbs, freeze-dried ones usually have the best flavour. For desserts, chocolate should contain at least 50 per cent cocoa solids – check the back of the wrapper.

> Some of the recipes contain raw or lightly cooked eggs. Because of the slight risk of salmonella poisoning, these should be avoided by the sick, the elderly, the very young, and pregnant women.
> The chances of contamination are greatly reduced if you buy free-range eggs, preferably organic, from a reputable supplier.

Many of the recipes in this book include wine. Use a wine that you would enjoy drinking rather than cheap 'cooking' wine – if it's not worth drinking it's not worth cooking with! You can use unsweetened apple juice or stock if you prefer.

The chefs on **Ready Steady Cook** often cook on a ridged grill pan. Ridged grill pans are made of cast iron and usually have a spout for pouring off the cooking juices. They are a very healthy way of cooking because the ridges keep the food raised above any fat that runs off. They also make attractive grill marks on food – to make a criss-cross pattern, give the food a half-turn half way through cooking each side. Use ridged grill pans for steaks, chops, fish or chunky slices of vegetables such as aubergines, courgettes or peppers.

Finally, **Ready Steady Cook** is all about putting together a delicious meal from whatever ingredients you have to hand. The recipes in this book are proof that some of the most memorable dishes are the ones that come about on the spur of the moment. So, if you don't have a particular ingredient, follow the example of our chefs and improvise. Don't be afraid to get in the kitchen and ***Ready Steady Cook!***

LARDER INGREDIENTS USED ON *READY STEADY COOK*

Arrowroot
Baking powder
Balsamic vinegar
Bay leaves
Beef stock cubes
Bottle of red wine
Bottle of white wine
Caster sugar
Cayenne pepper
Chicken stock cubes
Chilli powder
Cornflour
Demerara sugar
Dijon mustard
Double cream
Dried mixed herbs
Dried oregano
Eggs, size 3
Fresh basil
Fresh coriander
Fresh dill
Fresh parsley
Fresh rosemary
Fresh sage
Fresh thyme
Fresh white bread
Garam masala
Garlic

Golden syrup
Granulated sugar
Greek yoghurt
Ground all-spice
Ground cinnamon
Ground coriander
Ground ginger
Ground nutmeg
Honey
Lemons/Limes
Milk
Olive oil
Oranges
Plain flour
Red-wine vinegar
Self-raising flour
Sesame oil
Soft brown sugar
Soy sauce
Sunflower oil
Tabasco sauce
Tomato purée
Tomato sauce
Turmeric
Unsalted butter
Vegetable stock cubes
White-wine vinegar
Wholegrain mustard

VEGETARIAN DISHES

LESLEY WATERS

VEGGIES FOR VISHNU

Vegetable *tarte tatin* with tomato relish and vegetable fritters

Indira Ragubeer had only been in the UK for a year and was facing two problems. One was the cold weather and the other was her husband, Vishnu, who hated vegetables. Although Lesley managed to create something to change Vishnu's opinion of veggies, she couldn't help with changing the weather!

SERVES 2

FOR THE *TARTE TATIN*

Olive oil

1 large red pepper, seeded and sliced

1 large courgette, sliced

$1/2$ red onion, finely chopped

1 tablespoon chopped fresh parsley

225 g (8 oz) ready-to-roll shortcrust pastry

Salt and freshly ground black pepper

FOR THE RELISH

5 tomatoes, roughly chopped

2 garlic cloves, chopped

2 tablespoons chopped fresh coriander

$1/2$ red onion, finely chopped

Salt and freshly ground black pepper

FOR THE FRITTERS

Sunflower oil, for deep-frying

3 eggs, beaten

Plain flour

1 aubergine, sliced

1 courgette, sliced

Salt and freshly ground black pepper

Pre-heat the oven to gas mark 6, 200°C, 400°F. To make the vegetable *tarte tatin*, heat 2 tablespoons of the olive oil in a 23-cm frying-pan that you can also use in the oven (or use an ordinary frying pan and transfer to a loose bottomed cake tin after frying). Arrange the pepper, courgette and onion on the base of the pan. Sprinkle over the parsley and season with salt and pepper. Cook over a medium heat for 3–4 minutes.

On a lightly floured surface, roll out the pastry. Cut out a circle slightly larger than the base of the pan. Put the pastry on top of the vegetables, trim off any excess pastry and press it down gently with your fingers. Bake in the oven for about 15–18 minutes, or until the pastry is golden brown.

Meanwhile, to make the relish, put the tomatoes, garlic, coriander and onion in a food processor and process until smooth. Season with salt and pepper.

To make the fritters, heat the sunflower oil in a deep frying-pan or wok. Put the eggs in a shallow bowl and season them and put the flour on a plate and season it. Dip the aubergine and courgette slices in the egg and then coat them in the flour. Deep-fry them a few at a time, until they are golden and crisp. Drain them on kitchen paper and keep them warm until you are ready to serve.

Remove the tart from the oven and invert it on to a plate. Serve the vegetable fritters with the tomato relish separately.

READY STEADY COOK Tips

Always deep-fry ingredients a few at a time so they are not crowded in the pan. If you put in too many at once, you will reduce the temperature of the oil and the food will not crisp.

The original tarte tatin is made with apples, but you can apply the same upside-down principle to all sorts of interesting fruits or vegetables.

Coat the aubergines and courgettes with egg and flour only when you are ready to put them straight into the hot oil, otherwise they will go soggy.

You can make your own pastry, if you prefer, but the ready-to-roll versions in the chill cabinet or freezer at the supermarket are excellent quality and save a lot of time.

LESLEY WATERS

LAZY LASAGNE

Spinach and mushroom baked lasagne and open lasagne

Robin Ballance from London wanted a recipe for lasagne which, unlike his own, didn't taste like 'wallpaper paste'. Lesley obliged with not one but two lasagne ideas, using the classic combination for vegetarian lasagne of spinach and mushrooms.

SERVES 4
225 g (8 oz) fresh spinach
350 g (12 oz) fresh or pre-cooked lasagne sheets
200 ml (7 fl oz) olive oil
$1/_2$ onion, chopped
250 g (9 oz) chestnut mushrooms, sliced
Salt and freshly ground black pepper

FOR THE BAKED LASAGNE
150 ml (5 fl oz) double cream
1 tablespoon wholegrain French mustard

100 ml ($3^1/_2$ fl oz) white wine
25 g (1 oz) parmesan cheese, grated
100 g (4 oz) mozzarella cheese

FOR THE OPEN LASAGNE
Small handful of fresh basil
2 garlic cloves, peeled
1 tablespoon parmesan cheese, grated
1 teaspoon ground turmeric
 tablespoons chopped fresh flatleaf parsley
1 tablespoon lemon juice
1 tomato, sliced, to garnish

Pre-heat the oven to gas mark 7, 220°C, 425°F. Put two-thirds of the spinach in a saucepan, season with a little salt and pepper and put on the lid. Let the spinach cook in its own juices, until wilted. Drain and keep warm.

Cook the pasta sheets in a large pan of salted, boiling water, according to the packet instructions. Drain the pasta and refresh it in cold water.

Heat 2 tablespoons of the oil in a frying-pan. Add the onion and cook until softened. Add the mushrooms and cook for 2–3 more minutes. Season, put half the mixture in a bowl and keep warm.

To make the baked lasagne, add the cream, mustard and wine to the frying-pan and cook for 2 minutes.

Reserve half the lasagne sheets. Grease a small, shallow lasagne dish and put half of the remaining lasagne sheets to fit the base. Pour over half the sauce, scatter on a little parmesan and top with a layer of spinach. Repeat the layers of lasagne, mushroom, parmesan and spinach and then add the drained mozzarella cheese and remaining parmesan. Bake for 10–15 minutes, until golden brown.

To make the pesto for the open lasagne, put the basil and garlic in a food processor and chop them. Add 150 ml (5 fl oz) of the oil and the parmesan and process until the mixture is well blended and fairly finely chopped.

Heat the remaining oil in another frying-pan and add the turmeric and parsley. Halve the remaining pasta sheets and fry them for 1 minute, turning frequently until they are heated through.

To assemble the open lasagne, put a layer of fried pasta on a plate, pile on the reserved warm mushroom mixture and drizzle over half the pesto. Top with more pasta and pesto and garnish with slices of tomato. Serve the remaining spinach, shredded and flavoured with a little lemon juice and salt and pepper, separately.

READY STEADY COOK Tips

Pre-cooked lasagne sheets simply need to be rinsed in hot water before assembling the lasagne.

When warming the sauce in the pan, scrape up any oil and juices so that you retain all the flavour of the fried vegetables.

Freshly grated parmesan tastes better than the ready-grated tubs and, being a hard cheese, keeps fairly well. If you do have any left over, try grating it over steamed vegetables or sprinkling on soup.

LESLEY WATERS

READY, TEDDY, FETA

Filo roulade and feta toasties with salsa

If you go down to the woods today, you'll find Glaswegian teddy bear fanatic Chris Conran – a man fed up with meat dishes. He didn't come in disguise but he was certainly surprised by Lesley's delicious concoction of vegetables and feta cheese. He even brought his favourite teddy along for its own picnic!

SERVES 2–3
8 sheets of filo pastry
Olive oil

FOR THE FILLING
1 courgette, chopped
Juice of 1 lemon
185 g (6^1/$_2$ oz) tin of pitted black olives in brine, drained and chopped
200 g (7 oz) feta cheese
2 tomatoes, roughly chopped
^{1}/$_2$ red onion, roughly chopped
Handful of fresh basil leaves
Freshly ground black pepper

FOR THE TOASTIES
1 tablespoon olive oil
1 teaspoon ground turmeric
2 thick slices of country-style bread

FOR THE SALSA
2 tablespoons olive oil
1 courgette, sliced lengthways in thin strips
^{1}/$_2$ red onion, roughly chopped
2 garlic cloves, chopped
1 tablespoon chopped fresh parsley
2 tomatoes, roughly chopped
1 tablespoon balsamic vinegar
Pinch of sugar
Salt and freshly ground black pepper

Pre-heat the oven to gas mark 7, 220°C, 425°F. Put a clean tea towel on the work surface and lay six sheets of filo pastry on it, overlapping the sheets, to form a large rectangle. Brush the filo with olive oil.

In a bowl, mix together the courgette, lemon juice, half the olives, half the feta, crumbled, tomatoes and onion. Spread the mixture over the filo and scatter on most of the basil leaves, reserving a few of the best to garnish. Season with pepper. Using the tea towel, roll the filo into a cylinder. Put it on a greased baking sheet, in a horseshoe shape. If there are any cracks, patch them with the remaining filo. Brush with a little oil and bake for 15 minutes, or until the pastry is golden brown.

Gently heat the oil and the turmeric in a small frying-pan. Cut out two discs of bread, using a 5 cm (2 in) cutter. Fry the bread for 1–2 minutes, turning frequently, until golden and crisp. Place on a baking sheet. Cut the remaining feta in half and put a piece on each disc. Bake for 5 minutes, or until the feta is soft and starting to brown.

For the salsa, put a tablespoon of olive oil in another frying-pan and fry the courgette and onion until golden. Add the garlic, parsley, tomatoes, balsamic vinegar, sugar, remaining olives and another tablespoon of olive oil. Season with salt and pepper, allow to warm through and remove from the heat.

To serve, put a toastie on each plate and top with salsa. Garnish with reserved basil leaves. Serve the filo roulade separately.

READY STEADY COOK Tips

Frozen filo pastry is a wonderful standby to keep in the freezer. Defrost thoroughly before using, and keep any sheets you are about to use covered with a damp cloth while you are preparing a dish so that they do not dry out and become too crumbly to manage.

Make sure the oil is hot enough before adding the bread otherwise it will soak up too much oil. It should start to sizzle as soon as it enters the pan.

These filling ingredients will also make a delicious fresh salad.

K E V I N   W O O D F O R D

ANNIE'S ARTICHOKES WITH A BIT ON THE SIDE

Globe artichoke with two dressings and vegetable
hors d'oeuvre with two dressings

Rock-jiving Anne Taylor simply wanted to jive up her artichokes! Kevin came up with this idea
for artichokes with a mushroom and a cream dressing and also two dressings for a mixture of
vegetable hors d'oeuvre.

SERVES 4
Juice of 1 lemon
4 globe artichokes
Salt and freshly ground black pepper

FOR THE MUSHROOM DRESSING
100 g (4 oz) butter
3 garlic cloves, finely chopped
1 white onion, finely chopped
12 open-cup mushrooms, finely chopped
3 tablespoons brandy
3 tablespoons chopped fresh coriander

FOR THE CREAM DRESSING
6 egg yolks
350 g (12 oz) unsalted butter, melted
3 tablespoons double cream

FOR THE VINAIGRETTE DRESSING
6 tablespoons good olive oil
2 tablespoons white-wine vinegar
2 teaspoons French mustard

FOR THE PAPRIKA AND CREAM DRESSING
100 ml (4 fl oz) double cream
1 teaspoon paprika
Lemon juice

FOR THE HORS D'OEUVRE
1 apple
Juice of 1 lemon
1 large celeriac, peeled and grated
4 beetroot, peeled and chopped
1 white onion, finely chopped
2 tablespoons chopped fresh parsley
2 tablespoons chopped fresh coriander
8 carrots, grated
1 large mooli, peeled and grated

Heat a saucepan of water and add half the lemon juice. Remove the outer leaves from the artichokes, trim the base and remove the prickles, to leave the heart. Scoop out the centre, leaving a hollow. Put the artichokes in the pan and leave to simmer for about 20–25 minutes, or until the outside leaves will pull out easily. Remove, drain and set aside.

Meanwhile, melt the butter in a small saucepan and add the garlic, the onion and most of the mushrooms. Season with salt and pepper and cook until softened. Add the brandy and set alight, tilting the pan until the flames die down. Cook for a further 3–4 minutes. Add the coriander and immediately remove from the heat and spoon into the centre of the artichokes. Put on heatproof plates.

Pre-heat the grill to hot. Put the egg yolks in a glass bowl over a pan of simmering water (which should not touch the bottom of the bowl). Gradually add the butter and whisk continuously. Add the cream, pour over the artichokes and place under the grill for 4–5 minutes.

Mix together the ingredients for the vinaigrette dressing and season to taste. Do the same for the paprika and cream dressing, adding a good squeeze of lemon juice, to taste, with the salt and pepper.

Slice the apple and squeeze some of the lemon juice over the apple slices. Combine the celeriac and beetroot and toss in some of the vinaigrette dressing.

Add the onion, with the parsley and coriander, to the carrots. Toss in the remaining vinaigrette.

Add the reserved mushrooms to the mooli and toss in the cream and paprika dressing.

To serve, put each artichoke in the centre of a plate and alternate the apple, celeriac, carrot and mooli hors d'oeuvre around the edge.

KEVIN WOODFORD

DAWN'S DELIGHTFUL TIMBALES

Courgette timbales with tomato sauce and potato nests

Never having done anything with a vegetable apart from boil it, Dawn Adams thought it was about tiime she learnt to do more. These timbales are easy to do and thoroughly live up to their name.

SERVES 2

FOR THE TIMBALES
1 medium-sized courgette and
1 small courgette
1 tablespoon olive oil
50 g (2 oz) mushrooms, roughly chopped
150 g (5 oz) tomatoes, skinned, seeded and chopped
1 garlic clove, crushed
4 tablespoons white wine
50 g (2 oz) fresh breadcrumbs
$1/2$ teaspoon tomato purée
Salt and freshly ground black pepper
Sprigs of flatleaf parsley, to garnish

FOR THE POTATO NESTS
1 large baking potato
2 tablespoons double cream or milk
50 g (2 oz) Cheshire cheese, grated
Salt and freshly ground black pepper

FOR THE SAUCE
1 tablespoon olive oil
4 spring onions, finely sliced
75 g (3 oz) mushrooms, roughly chopped
150 g (5 oz) tomatoes, skinned, seeded and chopped
75 ml ($2^3/4$ fl oz) white wine
$1/2$ teaspoon tomato purée
Salt and freshly ground black pepper

Using a potato peeler, cut six thin, lengthways slices of courgette and blanch them in boiling water for 30 seconds. Refresh under cold water and set aside.

Chop the remaining courgettes. Heat the oil in a pan, add the courgettes, mushrooms, tomatoes and garlic and cook for a minute.

Add the wine, breadcrumbs and tomato purée and season with salt and pepper. Cook for 8–10 minutes.

Meanwhile, prick the potato skin with a sharp knife and microwave it on full power for 6–8 minutes, or until tender.

Line two timbale moulds or 10 cm (4 in) ramekin dishes with cling film. Line the moulds with courgette slices, leaving the ends of the slices to overhang the edges of the moulds. Fill with the courgette and mushroom mixture and bring the ends of the courgette slices back, to cover the filling. Cover with cling film to enclose courgettes and filling. Stand the moulds in a pan of barely simmering water (the water should come only halfway up the sides of the moulds) and poach for 5 minutes making sure the water does not bubble over the tops of the moulds.

To make the sauce, heat the oil in another pan, add the spring onions, mushrooms and tomatoes and cook for 3 minutes. Add the wine and tomato purée and season with salt and pepper. Cook for 4–5 minutes, stirring occasionally.

Pre-heat the grill to hot. Cut the potato in half and scoop out the flesh. Mash with the cream and season well. Pipe or spoon two 10 cm (4 in) nests on to flameproof serving plates. Alternatively, pipe or spoon the potato back into the skins. Sprinkle the cheese in the middle and grill for 2 minutes, until golden.

To serve, turn the timbales out on to serving plates and spoon the sauce around them. Garnish with flatleaf parsley and serve with the potato nests.

READY STEADY COOK Tips

Blanching the courgette slices makes them tender and flexible for lining the ramekins.

Microwave 'baked' potatoes are a wonderful standby for a quick and filling lunch. Top them with grated cheese and herbs, mix in some flaked tuna and mayonnaise, top with a spoonful of bolognaise sauce or stir in a little pesto.

ANGIE'S SUPER SUPPER SURPRISE

Semolina gnocchi with spicy tomato sauce

Single mum Angie Tindall wondered if the thing she hated most in the world – semolina – could actually be turned into something delicious. These delightful gnocchi – Italian-style dumplings – convinced her.

SERVES 2

FOR THE GNOCCHI
450 ml (15 fl oz) milk
75 g (3 oz) semolina
$1/2$ teaspoon grated nutmeg
1 egg yolk
25 g (1 oz) butter
1 tablespoon double cream
75 g (3 oz) parmesan cheese, grated
Salt and freshly ground black pepper

FOR THE SAUCE
15 g ($1/2$ oz) butter
$1/2$ onion, finely chopped
$1/2$ red pepper, seeded and sliced
$1/2$ leek, sliced
1 garlic clove, crushed
1 tablespoon chopped fresh coriander
1 tablespoon chopped fresh parsley
400 g (14 oz) tin of chopped tomatoes
Tabasco sauce
4 tablespoons tomato purée
Salt and freshly ground black pepper

To make the gnocchi, bring the milk to the boil and stir in the semolina, keeping the pan on the heat. The mixture will begin to thicken. Add the nutmeg and egg yolk, stirring continuously. Season with salt and pepper. Add the butter, cream and half the parmesan and mix thoroughly. Spoon the semolina into a small, shallow, buttered ovenproof dish and leave to cool while you make the sauce.

To make the sauce, melt the butter in a saucepan and sauté the onion, pepper, leek, garlic and herbs for 5 minutes. Add the tomatoes, 4–5 drops of Tabasco sauce and tomato purée and leave to simmer for 10 minutes, stirring occasionally. Add salt and pepper to season if required.

Pre-heat the grill to hot. Turn the semolina out and cut out circles from it, with a pastry cutter. Replace the rounds in the dish, sprinkle over the remaining parmesan and grill for 4–5 minutes until the cheese melts and turns golden brown.

To serve, place the gnocchi on a plate and surround with the sauce.

KEVIN WOODFORD

MEXICAN ROSINA

Spicy-bean tortillas with cheese and avocado cream

Gary, from Telford, told Kevin that he'd like something Mexican and something plentiful enough to satisfy his young daughter's appetite – 'She's a small lass but I've seen her devour a whole trout!'.

SERVES 4
6 large soft tortillas
Salt and freshly ground black pepper

FOR THE FILLING
2 tablespoons olive oil
1 garlic clove, crushed
1 small onion, finely chopped
400 g (14 oz) tin of chopped tomatoes
400 g (14 oz) tin of kidney beans, drained and rinsed
2 teaspoons Worcestershire sauce
1 tablespoon tomato purée
1 teaspoon chilli powder

5 tablespoons white wine
3–4 fresh basil leaves, chopped

FOR THE CHEESE SAUCE
40 g (1$^{1}/_{2}$ oz) butter
40 g (1$^{1}/_{2}$ oz) plain flour
600 ml (1 pint) milk
75 g (3 oz) mild Cheddar cheese, grated
Salt and freshly ground black pepper

FOR THE AVOCADO CREAM
1 avocado, peeled and stoned
150 ml (5 fl oz) double cream
Juice of $^{1}/_{2}$ lemon

Pre-heat the oven to gas mark 6, 200°C, 400°F. To make the filling, heat the oil in a saucepan and add the garlic, onion, tomatoes, kidney beans, Worcestershire sauce, tomato purée, chilli powder, wine and basil. Cook for 8–10 minutes.

To make the cheese sauce, melt the butter in a small pan and add the flour. Mix together for a minute or two and then gradually add the milk and stir until thickened and just bubbling. Off the heat, add the cheese, season and whisk until smooth.

Line a buttered, shallow, ovenproof dish with four tortillas. Make sure these are slightly overlapping the edge of the dish. Pour on the bean filling and then cover with remaining tortillas. Pour on the cheese sauce. Bake for 15 minutes.

For the dip, blend the avocado, cream, lemon juice and seasoning, using a fork or in a food processor. Serve as an accompaniment to the tortillas.

READY STEADY COOK Tip
Serve the avocado dip on its own, as a starter, with corn chips and/or crudités to dip in.

LESLEY WATERS

THE ITALIAN CONNECTION

Tuna pizzas with rustic bread and olive and mushroom salad

A designer of bank notes, Lionel Walker from Amersham failed to bring us any samples. Instead he wanted Lesley to show him the techniques of Italian cooking. Lesley obliged with these tuna pizzas and rustic-style bread and Lionel said the end result looked like 'an artist's palette'.

SERVES 2

280 g (about 10 oz) packet of bread mix
40 g ($1\frac{1}{2}$ oz) sun-dried tomatoes in oil
10-11 tablespoons warm water
2 tomatoes, skinned, seeded and chopped

185 g (about 7 oz) tin of tuna in brine, drained
4 tablespoons grated mozzarella cheese
2 tablespoons chopped fresh basil

FOR THE SALAD
2 eggs
5 tablespoons good olive oil
100 g (4 oz) button mushrooms
2 garlic cloves, crushed

juice of ¹/₂ lemon
1 tablespoon snipped fresh chives
¹/₂ cos lettuce
6 pitted green olives
Salt and freshly ground black pepper

Pre-heat the oven to gas mark 7, 220°C, 425°F. Put the bread mix in a food processor or mixing bowl, together with 2 tablespoons of oil from the sun-dried tomatoes and some water. Process or mix by hand, to form a soft dough. Knead for 3–4 minutes on a floured surface.

Halve the dough and roll out one half. Chop four of the sun-dried tomatoes and sprinkle them over the dough. Fold over the dough and re-roll it, to make a 23 cm (9 in) round. Score halfway through the dough, to expose the tomatoes, brush with a little more of their oil. Shape into a compact oval shape and put on a greased baking sheet.

Divide the remaining dough into two and roll out each piece, to make 18 cm (7 in) individual pizzas. Transfer the pizza bases to a greased baking sheet and spread a tablespoon of the chopped tomatoes over each. Sprinkle over a little of the tuna, 2 tablespoons of the cheese and any remaining sun-dried tomatoes on to each pizza.

Bake both trays of dough in the oven for 10 minutes, until brown and crisp. Sprinkle the chopped basil over the pizzas just before the end of cooking time. Brush the tomato bread with a tablespoon of the oil from the sun-dried tomatoes.

Meanwhile, hard-boil the eggs for 6–8 minutes, drain them and put them in cold, running water, to cool. Shell the eggs and quarter them.

Heat 2 tablespoons of the olive oil, add the mushrooms and garlic and sauté over medium heat, for 3–4 minutes.

To make the dressing, pour the remaining 3 tablespoons of olive oil into a bowl or jar, add the lemon juice, chives and salt and pepper to taste. Mix thoroughly. Pour over the mushrooms, to warm the dressing.

Tear the lettuce leaves into pieces and put them on a serving plate or in a bowl. Spoon over the remaining tuna and the egg quarters and olives and pour over the mushrooms and dressing just before serving. Serve the pizzas with the salad, and the rustic bread on a board.

FISH AND SHELLFISH

GET YOUR SKATES ON - 25

CRACKINGLY CRISP CONTAINERS
WITH COD STEAKS - 27

OUR PLAICE - 28

TEN TORS TUNA - 30

DANIELLA'S DELIGHTFUL DEEP-SEA PASTA - 31

AROMATIC FEAST - 32

BENNETT'S BASIL BISQUE AND
DRIGHLINGTON DELIGHT - 34

LORNA'S LUSCIOUS LOBSTER - 36

GLENN'S PAISLEY SURPRISE - 38

ANDREW'S FISH PIE - 40

SARAH'S MEDLEY OF FRESH FISH ON A BED OF
CHABLIS AND SPRING ONION SAUCE - 42

LESLEY WATERS

GET YOUR SKATES ON

Skate wing with black-butter sauce with capers, and fennel and potato rösti and warm salad

The office was flooded with fan mail after Norman Ellis came on the show and told Fern he was looking for a wife! He will be able to charm the lucky lady with this excellent fish recipe that's just right for two.

SERVES 2

FOR THE SKATE
100 ml (3¹/₂ fl oz) white wine
3 thyme sprigs
1 bay leaf
6 black peppercorns
Slice of lemon
1 tablespoon white-wine vinegar
2 skate wings

FOR THE RÖSTIS
1 large potato, peeled and coarsely grated
2 tablespoons olive oil
1 fennel bulb, quartered and sliced thinly
6 black peppercorns
Dried oregano
Freshly ground black pepper

FOR THE WARM SALAD
500 g (1 lb 2 oz) broccoli, cut in florets
1 tablespoon olive oil
1 yellow pepper, seeded and chopped
Small handful of basil leaves
Salt and freshly ground black pepper

FOR THE DRESSING
75 ml (2 ³/₄ fl oz) white wine
1 tablespoon olive oil
1 teaspoon Dijon mustard
1 tablespoon white-wine vinegar

FOR THE SAUCE
50 g (2 oz) unsalted butter
2 tablespoons caper
Lemon juice

Bring a saucepan and a shallow pan of water to the boil. Dry the grated potato in a tea towel.

Put the wine, thyme, bay leaf, black peppercorns, lemon slice and vinegar in the shallow pan with the water and bring back to a simmer for 4 minutes.

Meanwhile, make the röstis. Heat a tablespoon of the oil and gently fry the fennel and black peppercorns for about 8 minutes. In a bowl, mix together the fennel and potato. Add a good pinch of oregano and season with pepper. Set aside until cool enough to handle, then mould into two röstis (flat, pattie shapes). Heat the remaining oil in a small frying-pan and fry one rösti for 2–3 minutes, until golden brown underneath. Turn it by putting a baking tray on top and inverting the frying-pan. Repeat to brown the other side and then keep warm while you fry the second in the same way. While the röstis are frying add the fish to the shallow pan and poach gently for 10–12 minutes, turning once until firm and opaque. Keep the röstis warm while you make the salad.

For the salad, put the broccoli into the saucepan of boiling water and cook for about 3 minutes. Drain and refresh in cold water. Heat the oil in a wok and stir-fry the pepper and broccoli for 2–3 minutes until tender but still firm. Season. Mix together all the ingredients for the dressing, pour into the wok and add some basil leaves.

Melt the butter in a small frying-pan and cook the capers, with a squeeze of lemon juice, until the butter is dark. This takes about 4 minutes over high heat.

To serve, put the röstis and skate wings on two warmed plates and pour the caper sauce over the fish. Serve with the broccoli and pepper salad.

READY STEADY COOK Tips
Try making rösti with sliced onion and bacon to serve with continental sausages or grilled meats.

Frying the spices imparts a wonderful flavour to the frying oil.

Experiment with other spices for different flavour effects.
Like any fish, skate should be very fresh. It has a slight ammonia smell when it is past its best.

LESLEY WATERS

CRACKINGLY CRISP CONTAINERS WITH COD STEAKS

Cod steaks with aromatic stewed peppers, tomato and cheese filo parcels and roasted-tomato salad

On a programme broadcast near to Christmas, Huw Dennis said he was already fed up with the idea of turkey and spuds, so he presented Lesley with fish and pastry and asked her to come up with an original idea.

SERVES 2

FOR THE PEPPERS
2 tablespoons olive oil
$1/2$ green pepper, seeded and sliced
$1/2$ yellow pepper, seeded and sliced
1 garlic clove, crushed
1 tablespoon chopped fresh mixed herbs
$1/2$ lemon
Salt and freshly ground black pepper

1 tablespoon chopped fresh sage
4 filo pastry sheets
Salt and freshly ground black pepper

FOR THE SALAD
4 tomatoes, halved with cores removed
2 tablespoons olive oil
2 tablespoons chopped fresh basil
Salt and freshly ground black pepper

FOR THE FILO PARCELS
3 tablespoons olive oil
1 small onion, chopped
4 tomatoes, cut in wedges
50 g (2 oz) Cheddar cheese, grated

FOR THE COD
1 tablespoon olive oil
2 x 150 g (5 oz) cod steaks
4 tablespoons white wine
Salt and freshly ground black pepper

Pre-heat the oven to gas mark 6, 200°C, 400°F. To make the peppers, heat the oil in a pan, add the peppers, garlic and herbs and season with salt and pepper. Squeeze in the lemon juice and add the squeezed lemon half. Cover and cook gently for 15 minutes, stirring now and again.

Meanwhile, make the filo parcels. Heat a tablespoon of oil in another pan, add the onion and cook for 3 minutes. Add the tomatoes and cook for 2 minutes. Off the heat, stir in the cheese, sage and seasoning.

Cut each sheet of filo pastry in half to give two squares. Brush one square of filo pastry with a little oil and place another square on top. Spoon a quarter of the tomato and cheese mixture into the centre. Lift the corners of the filo over the filling and pinch the edges together, to seal and form a parcel. Put on a greased baking sheet and brush with 1 tablespoon of oil. Repeat with the remaining filo and filling, to make four parcels. Bake for 6–8 minutes, until golden brown.

To make the salad, put the tomato halves on a baking sheet. Drizzle the oil over them, scatter the chopped basil over the top and season well. Roast for 12–15 minutes, until the skins are lightly charred.

For the cod, heat the oil in a frying-pan, add the steaks, wine and seasoning and cook for 8 minutes, turning once.

To serve, spoon the peppers over the cod steaks (discarding the lemon half) and serve with the filo parcels. Serve on a plate with the roasted tomato salad, garnished with basil leaves.

L E S L E Y   W A T E R S

OUR PLAICE

Pan-fried plaice fillets and tartare sauce, with grilled courgettes, potatoes and petits pois

Philip Singh wanted to be treated to a fish dish because his wife, Corrine, hates fish and so he has to go without it at home.

SERVES 2

FOR THE COURGETTES
2 courgettes, sliced lengthways
1 tablespoon olive oil
juice of $\frac{1}{2}$ lemon

Salt and freshly ground black pepper

FOR THE POTATOES
225 g (8 oz) potatoes, cut in
2 cm ($\frac{3}{4}$ in) chunks

100 g (4 oz) petits pois or peas
3 tablespoons olive oil
15 g ($^1/_2$ oz) sun-dried tomatoes, chopped
2 tablespoons chopped fresh dill
Salt and freshly ground black pepper

FOR THE PLAICE
3 shallots, quartered
1 medium-size plaice, cut in 4 fillets and skinned
Plain flour

25 g (1 oz) unsalted butter
Salt and freshly ground black pepper

FOR THE SAUCE
100 g (4 oz) Greek yoghurt
1 tablespoon gherkins, chopped
1 tablespoon capers, chopped
Salt and freshly ground black pepper

TO GARNISH
Chopped fresh parsley
Orange wedges

Pre-heat the grill to hot. Mix the oil and the lemon juice in a small bowl and season with salt and pepper. Dip the courgette slices in the marinade to coat. Then place them on the grill rack and grill for 12–15 minutes, turning once, until well browned, brushing with marinade halfway through cooking.

Meanwhile, cook the potatoes in boiling water for 8–10 minutes, or until tender.

Now begin cooking the plaice. Melt the butter in a large frying-pan and cook the shallots for 3 minutes, stirring occasionally.

Lightly dust the fillets with flour and season well. Add the fillets to the pan and fry for 3–4 minutes, turning once, until golden.

Cook the petits pois for 3 minutes. Drain the potatoes and peas and put in a serving bowl. Add the oil, sun-dried tomatoes, dill and seasoning and toss until well mixed.

Mix the Greek yoghurt, gherkins, capers and seasoning, to make a tartare sauce. Spoon into a serving bowl.

To serve, put the fillets on warmed serving plates, scatter the shallots over the top and arrange the courgettes to one side. Sprinkle the parsley over the fish and shallots and garnish with orange wedges. Serve the potatoes and peas and the tartare sauce separately.

LESLEY WATERS

TEN TORS TUNA

Griddled tuna steak, with roasted tomatoes, cardamom beans and cheese-and-mustard potatoes

Busy training youngsters for The Ten Tors, Pat Read, from Exeter, needed something quick, easy and healthy. She brought along some Curworthy cheese, a local Okehampton favourite, with a unique flavour but mature Cheddar works just as well.

SERVES 2–3

FOR THE POTATOES
25 g (1 oz) butter
$^1/_2$ onion, finely chopped
900 g (2 lb) new potatoes, washed and thickly sliced
2 bay leaves
150 ml (5 fl oz) white wine
450 ml (15 fl oz) vegetable stock
150 g (5 oz) mature Cheddar cheese, grated
1 tablespoon Dijon mustard
Salt and freshly ground black pepper

FOR THE TOMATOES
5 large plum tomatoes
$^1/_2$ onion, sliced
$^1/_2$ teaspoon chopped fresh thyme leaves
2 tablespoons olive oil
1 teaspoon Worcestershire sauce

FOR THE TUNA
2 tablespoons olive oil
1 tablespoon soy sauce
350 g (12 oz) tuna steak
Salt and freshly ground black pepper

FOR THE BEANS
150 g (5 oz) green beans
5 green cardamom pods
1 tablespoon olive oil

Pre-heat the oven to gas mark 6, 200°C, 400°F. Melt the butter in a large pan and add the onion and potatoes. Add the bay leaves, season with salt and pepper and sauté for 2 minutes. Add the wine and stock, cover and leave to simmer until the potatoes are tender, about 10–15 minutes. Make sure the pan does not dry out.

Meanwhile, put the tomatoes and sliced onion in a bowl and add the thyme, oil and Worcestershire sauce. Stir well, place on a baking sheet and roast for 12 minutes, until skins are lightly charred.

Mix the oil, soy sauce and seasoning and coat the tuna steak in the mixture. Heat a griddle pan or large, heavy-based frying-pan over very high heat. Griddle the tuna for 2–3 minutes on each side, until seared and cooked through. Cut the tuna into four steaks.

Meanwhile, blanch the beans in boiling water for 3 minutes. Drain and refresh under cold water. Cut in half. Crush the cardamom pods and extract the seeds. Heat the oil in a sauté pan and add the beans and the cardamom seeds. Allow to warm through.

Add the cheese and mustard to the potatoes and remaining stock. Stir to coat the potatoes and leave them in the covered pan until the cheese has melted. To serve, spoon the potatoes on a plate, top with the tuna steak and pile the tomatoes and beans around.

KEVIN WOODFORD

DANIELLA'S DELIGHTFUL DEEP-SEA PASTA

Pasta spirals in creamy seafood and tomato sauce, with grilled mussels and herby breadcrumbs

Before getting married, Kelly Gatta had never cooked, so she needed some help, particularly with seafood, which does need careful handling.

SERVES 2
175 g (6 oz) pasta twists
FOR THE SAUCE
2 tablespoons olive oil
8 raw tiger prawns, heads removed, shelled, shells reserved and bodies cut in
1 cm (½ in) chunks
10 cooked green-lipped New Zealand mussels, 4 shelled and chopped
10 medium tomatoes, quartered
150 ml (5 fl oz) red wine

2 tablespoons chopped fresh coriander
5 squid, cleaned and cut in rings
2 tablespoons double cream

FOR THE HERBY BREADCRUMBS
¼ small baguette
2 tablespoons chopped fresh basil
2 tablespoons chopped fresh parsley
2 tablespoons snipped fresh chives
1 garlic clove, crushed
2 tablespoons olive oil

Cook the pasta in salted, boiling water, according to the packet instructions. When cooked, drain and keep warm, tossed in a little oil, if necessary.

Meanwhile, to make the sauce, first heat a tablespoon of oil in a small pan and cook the prawn shells, four mussel shells, tomatoes, wine and coriander for 5 minutes. Remove the prawn and mussel shells and leave the sauce to simmer for a further 10 minutes. Liquidize the sauce and then pass it through a sieve.

Sauté the squid rings and prawns in the remaining oil for 2 minutes. Add the shelled mussels and the drained pasta and cook for a further minute. Add the tomato sauce and cream and mix thoroughly.

To make the grilled mussels, pre-heat the grill to hot. Put the bread, basil, parsley, chives and garlic in a food processor and process to fine crumbs. Slowly pour in the oil and mix well. Spread the herby breadcrumbs on the mussels in their shells and grill for 3–4 minutes, or until lightly golden brown.

Divide the pasta and sauce between two warmed serving dishes and garnish with the grilled mussels.

LESLEY WATERS

AROMATIC FEAST

Creamy fish curry with savoury rice and spicy green beans

Single and in search of a date, John Llewellyn asked Lesley for some culinary tips to impress the ladies. We are sure that no one could resist this wonderful and healthy fish curry.

SERVES 2	450 ml ($^3/_4$ pint) water
FOR THE RICE	2–3 bay leaves
1 tablespoon olive oil	1 lime, very finely chopped, including the skin
1 onion, chopped	Salt and freshly ground black pepper
150 g (5 oz) basmati rice, washed	

Above: Sar _____ ___ __ __ __ __ of Chablis

FOR THE CURRY
2 tablespoons sunflower oil
1 onion, chopped
2 green chillies, seeded if wished and finely chopped
2 tablespoons finely chopped fresh root ginger
1 teaspoon ground turmeric
1 tablespoon garam masala
1 teaspoon curry powder
150 ml (5 fl oz) white wine

150 ml (5 fl oz) water or vegetable stock
2 coley fillets, skinned and cut in
2.5 cm (1 in) pieces
4 tablespoons curd cheese
2 tablespoons hot water

FOR THE BEANS
150 g (5 oz) green beans
1 tablespoon sunflower oil
$1/2$ tablespoon garam masala
Coriander leaves, to garnish (optional)

To make the rice, heat the oil in a high-sided pan and sauté the onion for 4 minutes, or until it is translucent and soft. Add the rice and stir to coat it completely in oil. Pour in enough water to cover the rice, add the bay leaves and bring to the boil. Leave the rice covered to simmer until it has absorbed all the water. Stir in the lime just before serving. Season to taste.

For the fish curry, heat the oil and fry the onion until soft. Add the chillies and continue to cook for a minute. Then add the ginger, turmeric, garam masala and curry powder. Stir to make sure all the spices are coated in the oil. Pour in the wine and water or stock, bring to the boil and leave to simmer for 5 minutes, stirring occasionally.

Add the coley to the sauce and cook gently until the fish becomes firm and turns white, about 4–5 minutes.

Mix together the curd cheese and water. Stir the cheese into the fish curry and cook over a medium heat for a minute. Add extra water or stock if the sauce becomes too thick.

For the spicy beans, cook the beans in salted, boiling water for 5 minutes. Drain the beans. Heat the oil in a sauté or small frying-pan, add the beans and garam masala and cook for 2–3 minutes.

To serve, spoon the rice on to a large platter. Arrange the fish curry around the rice and garnish with fresh coriander leaves, if you like. Serve the beans separately.

KEVIN WOODFORD

BENNETT'S BASIL BISQUE AND DRIGHLINGTON DELIGHT

Simple paella, and basil and prawn bisque with garlic croûtons

Val Bennett had a dilemma: what on earth was she going to do with the neglected jar of artichokes in her cupboard? *Ready Steady Cook* and Kevin came up with the perfect answer.

SERVES 4

FOR THE PAELLA
2 tablespoons extra-virgin olive oil
350 g (12 oz) long-grain rice
1 slice of onion
Bunch of spring onions, chopped, green tops reserved
Small piece of fresh red chilli, seeded and chopped
1 red pepper, seeded and chopped
1/2 courgette, chopped
1 teaspoon ground turmeric
1 skinless, boneless chicken thigh, cut into 4 cm (1 1/2 in) cubes
1 garlic clove, crushed
350 g (12 oz) frozen peas
1 jar seasoned artichoke hearts, drained or
1 can artichoke hearts, drained
600 ml (1 pint) water
200 g (7 oz) cooked peeled prawns
150 g (5 oz) cooked shell-on prawns, heads removed and reserved
Salt and freshly ground black pepper

FOR THE BISQUE
2 tablespoons olive oil
1 tablespoon chopped fresh basil
1 tablespoon snipped fresh chives
1 slice of onion
1 garlic clove, crushed
75 g (3 oz) long-grain rice
2 tablespoons tomato purée
1.5 litres (2 1/2 pints) vegetable stock
300 ml (10 fl oz) white wine
Salt and freshly ground black pepper

FOR THE CROÛTONS
25 g (1 oz) butter
1 garlic clove, crushed
2 slices of bread, cubed

To make the paella, heat the oil in a deep saucepan. Add the rice, onion slice, the white of spring onion, chilli, pepper and courgette. Stir in the turmeric, chicken and garlic. Mix together and add the peas and artichokes. Pour in the water, stir well and bring just back to the boil. Season with salt and pepper. Leave to cook on a fairly low heat, until the rice has absorbed all the liquid. To check that the chicken is cooked, pierce with a skewer or sharp knife. If the juices run clear, the chicken is cooked.

To make the bisque, heat the oil in a saucepan. Put in the reserved prawn heads and green of spring onion, and the basil, chives, onion slice, garlic, rice, half the tomato purée, water and wine. Season and leave to reduce over a gentle heat for 15–20 minutes.

For the croûtons, melt the butter and add the garlic and bread cubes. Toss for 1–2 minutes until golden, drain on kitchen paper and keep warm.

Remove the prawn heads from the bisque, liquidize and pass it through a sieve. Return to the pan and add the remaining tomato purée. Heat through and season.

Stir the peeled prawns into the paella and cook for 2–3 minutes, to warm them through. Spoon the paella into a warmed serving dish and garnish it with the prawn tails. Pour the bisque into warmed soup bowls and garnish with the croûtons. Serve immediately.

READY STEADY COOK Tips
Cooked prawns only need to be warmed through in the paella. If you want to use uncooked prawns, cook them for a few minutes – just until they turn pink.

Paella can be made with a wide variety of ingredients, so if you have anything missing from your list or want to try making it with a different set of ingredients, there's no rules as long as it tastes good.

LORNA'S LUSCIOUS LOBSTER

Lobster in wine and cream sauce, with herby savoury rice

Lorna adored lobster but could never justify cooking it for herself until she was given one by a friendly local fisherman. Kevin added a delicious herby rice and a luxurious sauce for a fitting accompaniment to our most luxurious seafood.

SERVES 2	FOR THE LOBSTER
FOR THE RICE	1 medium cooked lobster
1 tablespoon olive oil	25 g (1 oz) butter
2 shallots, finely chopped	1 garlic clove, crushed
100 g (4 oz) long-grain rice	85 ml (3 fl oz) white wine
2 tablespoons chopped fresh dill	2 teaspoons Dijon mustard
1 tablespoon chopped fresh coriander	3 tablespoons double cream
1 tablespoon chopped fresh basil	Lemon juice
1 vegetable stock cube, dissolved in	1 egg yolk
850 ml (1½ pints) water	Lemon wedges, to garnish

To make the savoury rice, heat the oil in a heavy pan or frying-pan and fry a tablespoon of shallot for a minute. Add the rice and stir to coat it in oil. Mix the herbs together and add 2 tablespoons of herbs to the pan; stir and cook for another minute. Pour in the stock, bring to the boil and then leave to simmer on a low heat for 12–15 minutes, or until the rice has absorbed all the stock. Spoon the cooked rice into a large buttered ramekin dish.

Meanwhile, lay the lobster on its back and cut it in half from head to tail. Discard the stomach sac and intestinal tract. Scoop out all the white tail meat from both halves of the body, including the green meat. Wash and dry the shells. Cut off the legs and claws and remove as much meat as possible from them.

Melt the butter in a small, heavy pan and sauté the garlic and the rest of the shallots and herbs. Pour in the wine and bring to the boil. Add the mustard and cream and leave to simmer for 3 minutes. Add the lobster meat and a squeeze of lemon juice. Cook for another minute to heat the meat through, then stir in the egg yolk. Be careful not to let the sauce boil at this point, or it will curdle.

To serve, spoon the lobster flesh and sauce back into the half shells. Turn out the rice on to a warmed serving dish, in a neat mound. Garnish with lemon wedges.

READY STEADY COOK Tips

Lobster is delicious but, for a cheaper alternative, buy a cooked, dressed crab and take all the meat out of the shell. Add to the sauce as for the lobster and serve piled back into the shell, with the savoury rice.

Crack the lobster claws firmly with the back of a knife to lift out the meat.

Shallots have a more delicate flavour than onions. They should be gently softened in the pan and not allowed to brown.

Any left-over rice can be served cold as a salad.

GLENN'S PAISLEY SURPRISE

Haddock mousses with white wine and cream sauce and baby vegetables

Having recently given birth to Glenn, Lorraine Corrigan, from Paisley, was keen to find an infallible recipe that she could whip up at any hour! The sauce for the dish is a variation of the classic French *beurre blanc*.

SERVES 2

FOR THE MOUSSES
225 g (8 oz) haddock fillet, skinned
1 egg white
2 tablespoons double cream
1/2 tablespoon snipped fresh chives
Handful of spinach leaves
Grated zest of 1/2 lemon
Grated zest of 1/2 lime
Salt and freshly ground black pepper

FOR THE SAUCE
150 ml (5 fl oz) white wine
2 tablespoons double cream
2 tablespoons snipped fresh chives
50 g (2 oz) unsalted butter, chopped

TO SERVE
2 carrots cut *à la Parisienne*
(see tip)
5 French beans, sliced diagonally
1 tablespoon olive oil
5 baby onions or shallots
85 ml (3 fl oz) chicken stock

Put the fish in a food processor and add the egg white. Process for a minute. Add 2 tablespoons of cream, a little at a time to ensure that it doesn't curdle. Add the chives and season with salt and pepper.

Soften the spinach leaves in boiling water for 2 minutes. Drain under cold running water.

Butter two ramekin dishes and line them with cling film. Line the dishes with the spinach leaves. Divide the lemon and lime zest between each. Spoon in the fish-mousse mixture. Half-fill a roasting tin with boiling water and put the ramekins in it, making sure the water comes no more than halfway up the sides of the dishes. Cook the mousses at a simmer for 15–20 minutes, or until the mousse mixture is firm to the touch and heated through.

To make the sauce, first reduce the wine by half. This takes 4–5 minutes over a high heat. Add 2 tablespoons of cream and the chives. Whisk in the butter, piece by piece, and cook for a further 2 minutes until the sauce is thick and creamy.

Cook the carrots in salted, boiling water for 4–5 minutes, add the beans and cook for a further 2–3 minutes until *al dente* (tender but still with a slight bite in the middle).

Heat the oil in a small frying-pan and sauté the baby onions for 2 minutes until lightly coloured. Add the chicken stock, cover and cook for 5 minutes until the onions are soft and translucent. Drain the onions and mix them with the carrots and beans.

To serve, turn out each mousse on to a serving plate. Arrange the vegetables on one side and surround everything with the sauce.

READY STEADY COOK Tips

To make carrots à la Parisienne, cut the carrots into squarish chunks and use a swivel vegetable peeler to shave off the corners to make little balls. Alternatively, cut peeled carrots into 4 cm (1½ in) chunks, then use a melon baller to scoop out balls of carrot.

Use small, tender spinach leaves if you can. If they have a thickish stem, hold the stem in your right hand and fold the leaf in half, with the veins outwards, with your left. Gently pull the stem upwards and it will pull away from the leaf.

Boiling a liquid to reduce it concentrates the flavours.

ANDREW'S FISH PIE

Cod in a creamy sauce, baked in filo pastry and served with mushroom sauce

With a strange addiction to fish-finger sandwiches (something that even his son Andrew finds disgusting), Dave Whittingham decided it was time to get 'posh with fish'.

SERVES 2

FOR THE PIE

75 g (3 oz) butter
50 g (2 oz) plain flour
300 ml (10 fl oz) milk
300 g (11 oz) cod fillet, skinned and cut in 1 cm (1/2 in) cubes
1 tablespoon olive oil
2 carrots, finely chopped
1 leek, thinly sliced
1 lemon grass stalk, thinly sliced
1 fresh red chilli, seeded and finely chopped
1 tablespoon chopped fresh dill
1 tablespoon chopped fresh flatleaf parsley
2 tablespoons chopped fresh basil
1 tablespoon white wine
Juice of 1/2 lemon
Salt and freshly ground black pepper
4 filo pastry sheets

FOR THE MUSHROOM SAUCE

25 g (1 oz) butter
1 tablespoon white wine
100 g (4 oz) mushrooms, sliced
2 tablespoons double cream
Salt and freshly ground black pepper

Pre-heat the oven to gas mark 6, 200°C, 400°F. Melt the butter in a small pan and keep it warm.

To make the white sauce, put 5 tablespoons of the melted butter in another saucepan, add the flour, stir well and cook for 30 seconds. Slowly add the milk, stirring continuously, and bring to the boil. Off the heat, add a cube of cod and leave for the flavour to infuse.

Heat the oil and sauté the carrots, leek, lemon grass, chilli and herbs, until the carrots are soft. Stir in the wine and then add the white sauce and lemon juice and season with salt and black pepper.

Brush the filo pastry sheets with some of the remaining melted butter. Put them one on top of the other in a greased, round, ovenproof dish, letting the pastry edges fall over the side of the dish. Put the cubes of cod on the pastry, pour over the sauce and fold the edges of the pastry back over the filling. Brush the top with the remaining butter and bake for 15 minutes, until the cod is cooked.

Heat the butter and wine and sauté the mushrooms in the mixture until softened. Stir in the cream and season to taste. Transfer to a warmed serving bowl.

Serve the fish pie straight from the oven, from the cooking dish, and hand round the mushroom sauce separately.

READY STEADY COOK Tips

If your sauce goes lumpy while you are adding the milk, take it off the heat and whisk it thoroughly until all the lumps have gone. Then return it to a gentle heat and stir well until cooked.

You can substitute any firm-fleshed white fish for this recipe: try roughy or ling.

If you can buy some wild mushrooms and sauté them lightly to serve with the dish.

SARAH'S MEDLEY OF FRESH FISH ON A BED OF CHABLIS AND SPRING ONION SAUCE

Poached fish with a simple *beurre blanc* sauce, served with herb and prawn croûtons, carrots and spring onions

Sarah's last attempt at fish had been a tuna lasagne, which had ended up on the floor, so she definitely needed some help with cooking simple fish dishes.

SERVES 2

FOR THE CROÛTONS
1 small baguette
Handful of fresh coriander
Handful of fresh parsley
Handful of fresh dill
2 tablespoons olive oil
75 g (3 oz) cooked, peeled prawns
75 g (3 oz) shell-on cooked prawns

200 g (7 oz) cod fillet, skin reserved and cut lengthways in half
200 g (7 oz) huss, bone removed, cut lengthways in half
$1/2$ lemon, sliced

FOR THE SAUCE
50 g (2 oz) unsalted butter, cubed
3 tablespoons double cream

FOR THE FISH MEDLEY
175 ml (6 fl oz) water
5 carrots, cut into batons, trimmings reserved
Bunch of spring onions, green tops reserved
3 tablespoons Chablis or other white wine

TO GARNISH
4 tomatoes, skinned, halved, seeded and chopped
1 slice of lemon
Chopped fresh parsley

Make the croûtons first. Pre-heat the grill. Slice half the baguette and toast both sides of the slices. Roughly chop the remaining baguette. Chop enough coriander leaves to make a tablespoon of chopped herb and set aside. Put the chopped bread, whole coriander leaves, parsley, dill, oil and peeled prawns in a food processor and process to a smooth paste. Divide and spread on each slice of toasted baguette.

Put the water in a shallow saucepan, add some of the carrot trimmings, the spring onion tops, chopped coriander, wine, fish skins and lemon slices and simmer for about 4 minutes (remove the fish skins after the first minute). Add the huss and cod and cover the pan with a circle of greaseproof paper, if you don't have a lid. Poach for 4 minutes. Remove the fish and keep it warm.

To make the sauce, strain the stock through a fine nylon sieve and reduce it for 2 minutes. Add the butter and cream, stirring constantly until the sauce thickens.

Meanwhile, cook the carrots in salted, boiling water for 6 minutes, add the whole spring onions and cook for 2–3 minutes more. Drain.

To serve, arrange the herb and prawn croûtons on warmed serving plates and put the fish in the middle. Pour the sauce over the fish and garnish with a shell-on prawn, tomatoes, a curled lemon slice and chopped fresh parsley. Serve the carrots and spring onions to the side.

READY STEADY COOK Tips

To skin tomatoes, make a slit in the top of each and put them in a bowl. Pour on boiling water to cover and leave for 10 seconds. Drain and remove the skins, which will peel away easily from the slit. Remove seeds with a teaspoon. Cut away core with a sharp knife and chop the flesh.

When poaching fish, keep the heat very low so that the liquid just scarcely bubbles on the surface. Never overcook the fish or you will lose the tender, succulent texture.

To store fresh parsley, wash the sprigs and pat them dry. Place them in a polythene bag, tied very loosely, and store in the bottom of the fridge for a few days.

POULTRY AND GAME

44

L E S L E Y   W A T E R S

RED HOT AND SPICY

Spicy turkey Stroganoff, turkey escalopes in dill sauce and courgette rice

Lorry driver Abdul had recently broken his leg during a rugby match and had become addicted to watching *Ready Steady Cook* from his sick bed. He told Lesley that he loved his food and especially loved it hot. This spicy turkey stroganoff could be as hot as you like, depending on the curry powder you use.

SERVES 3–4

6 x 100 g (4 oz) turkey breast steaks

FOR THE TURKEY STROGANOFF
2 tablespoons sunflower oil
1/2 onion, chopped
1 tablespoon curry powder
1 teaspoon ground turmeric
1 red pepper, seeded and sliced
2 tablespoons white wine
150 ml (5 fl oz) chicken stock
2 tablespoons tomato purée

FOR THE ESCALOPES
1 tablespoon olive oil
15 g (1/2 oz) butter
1/2 onion, chopped
1 tablespoon plain flour
4 tablespoons white wine
Grated zest and juice of 1 large orange
150 ml (5 fl oz) double cream
2 tablespoons chopped fresh dill
Salt and freshly ground black pepper

FOR THE RICE
200 g (7 oz) long-grain rice
25 g (1 oz) butter
1 large courgette, chopped
1 teaspoon ground turmeric
1 tablespoon chopped fresh coriander
1 tablespoon chopped fresh parsley
Salt and freshly ground black pepper
Dill sprigs, to garnish

Cook the rice in plenty of salted water, until tender. Drain and reserve. Meanwhile, slice three of the turkey steaks in thin strips. Heat the oil in a large frying-pan and sauté the onion, until soft. Add the curry powder and turmeric and fry for 30 seconds. Stir in the pepper and turkey and stir-fry for 3 minutes. Add the wine, stock and tomato purée and cook until the turkey is cooked through (no longer pink in the middle).

For the escalopes, heat the oil in another frying-pan and add the butter. Sauté the onion, until softened.

Put the other three turkey steaks between two sheets of cling film and beat them with a rolling-pin, to flatten them. Put the flour on a plate and season it. Dip the turkey in the flour to coat both sides. Add to the pan with the onion and fry for 3–4 minutes on each side. Add the wine, orange zest and juice and simmer for a minute. Stir in the cream and dill and season to taste. Bubble over a high heat for 1 minute and add a splash of water or stock if the sauce is too thick.

Melt the butter in a large pan and gently sauté the courgette for 2 minutes. Add turmeric. Stir in the drained rice and herbs. Season well.

To serve both dishes, tip the rice into cups or ramekin dishes (one per person) and invert them on to warmed plates. The stroganoff or the escalopes can be served alongside this mound of rice, garnished with dill sprigs.

L E S L E Y   W A T E R S

FOR PETE'S SAKE

Paella with chicken-stuffed roasted peppers

Peter Eblett admitted to being incredibly impatient in the kitchen and simply wanted to create something tasty in as little time as possible.

SERVES 4
FOR THE PAELLA
2 tablespoons olive oil
1 onion, chopped
1 fennel bulb, chopped
2 garlic cloves, crushed
450 g (1 lb) boneless, skinless chicken breast, cut in 1 cm ($^1/_2$ in) cubes

350 g (12 oz) long-grain rice
1 teaspoon ground turmeric
100 ml ($3^1/_2$ fl oz) white wine
600 ml (1 pint) vegetable or chicken stock
1 lime, grated rind and juice
1 tablespoon chopped fresh parsley
Salt and freshly ground black pepper

FOR THE PEPPERS
1 red pepper, halved and seeded
1 green pepper, halved and seeded
2 tablespoons olive oil
400 g (14 oz) tin of chopped tomatoes
Salt and freshly ground black pepper

FOR THE DRESSING
3 tablespoons olive oil
2 tablespoons white-wine vinegar
2 tablespoons chopped fresh parsley
1 teaspoon mustard
2 teaspoons water
Salt and freshly ground black pepper

Pre-heat the oven to gas mark 6, 200°C, 400°F. Heat the oil in a pan, add the onion, three-quarters of the fennel, the garlic and half the chicken and season with salt and pepper. Cook for 4 minutes. Stir in the rice and turmeric and add the wine and stock. Cover and simmer for 10–15 minutes, until the liquid has been absorbed and the rice is tender. Check regularly and add more stock if it dries out.

Meanwhile, put the pepper halves, cut side down, on a baking sheet and brush them with a tablespoon of oil. Roast for 10 minutes.

Heat the remaining tablespoon of oil in a pan, add the rest of the fennel and chicken and cook for 4 minutes. Add the tomatoes, season and leave to simmer for 5 minutes.

Meanwhile, make the dressing. Put the oil in a bowl with the vinegar, parsley, mustard, water and salt and pepper. Whisk together and pour over the peppers.

Spoon the chicken and tomato mixture into the roasted peppers.

Stir the lime juice and rind into the paella, with the parsley. Transfer to warmed serving plates and serve with the roasted peppers.

LESLEY WATERS

BACKPACKERS' FEAST

Cinnamon-spiced chicken casserole with hoummos, served with couscous cooked with carrot and onion

As she was soon to be travelling around the world on a tight budget, Ruth Lloyd saw her fiver budget as a real challenge. She sped around her local supermarket, determined to buy as many ingredients as possible. And didn't she do well! Lesley rose magnificently to the occasion with this interesting combination of casserole, couscous and hoummos.

SERVES 2–3

FOR THE COUSCOUS
200 g (7 oz) couscous
1 tablespoon olive oil
$\frac{1}{2}$ onion, chopped
3 carrots, chopped
Coriander leaves, to garnish

FOR THE CASSEROLE
2 tablespoons olive oil
$\frac{1}{2}$ onion, chopped
375 g (13 oz) skinless, boneless chicken thighs, cut in strips
2 teaspoons ground cinnamon
2 garlic cloves, crushed
1 aubergine, cubed

1 courgette, cubed
2 tablespoons tomato purée
200 ml (7 fl oz) white wine
200 ml (7 fl oz) chicken stock or water

FOR THE HOUMMOS
400 g (14 oz) tin of chick-peas, rinsed and drained
150 ml (5 fl oz) Greek yoghurt
1 garlic clove, crushed
2 tablespoons chopped fresh coriander
1 orange, halved
Olive oil
Salt and freshly ground black pepper
Coriander leaves, to garnish

Soak the couscous in plenty of boiling water for 10 minutes. Strain through a sieve, place the sieve over a large pan of simmering water, cover and leave to steam for 6–10 minutes.

Meanwhile, make the casserole. Heat the oil in a large pan and sauté the onion for 3 minutes, until softened. Add the chicken and cook, stirring, until sealed on all sides. Add the cinnamon, garlic, aubergine and courgette, stirring constantly. Add the tomato purée and wine and leave to cook for 15–20 minutes, stirring occasionally and adding a little water or chicken stock if necessary.

To garnish the couscous, heat the oil in a pan, add the onion and the carrots and cook slowly for 4–5 minutes until tender.

For the hoummos, put half the chick-peas into a blender or food processor, with the yoghurt, garlic and coriander, and the juice of half the orange. Blend or process to a soft consistency. Season to taste.

Cut the remaining half-orange into segments, spoon the hoummos on to a serving plate and spoon the reserved chick-peas and orange segments round the outside. Drizzle over a little olive oil, sprinkle with a little pepper and a few fresh coriander leaves, to garnish.

Tip the couscous out of the sieve on to a plate in a mound, spoon the cooked carrot and onion on top and garnish with coriander. Serve the casserole in a dish.

L E S L E Y   W A T E R S

MACCLESFIELD TEX MEX

Turkey chilli with tortillas, with turkey patties

Rugby-playing Peter Ord was fed up with the boring food he and the lads were being served after matches and wanted an idea for something more exciting: 'It's especially important if we lose ... again'. Chilli con carne made with turkey mince was definitely a winning tackle.

SERVES 2

FOR THE CHILLI
1 tablespoon olive oil
1/2 onion, finely chopped
350 g (12 oz) turkey mince
1 teaspoon ground cumin
1 teaspoon flour
2 teaspoons paprika
1 teaspoon tomato purée

3 tablespoons red wine
300 ml (10 fl oz) chicken stock
1/2 Habanero or small red chilli, seeded and finely chopped
Salt and freshly ground black pepper

FOR THE PATTIES
Slice of white country-style bread
1 tablespoon roughly chopped fresh coriander

$^1/_2$ Habanero or small red chilli, seeded
1 egg yolk
1 tablespoon olive oil

FOR THE DRESSING
3 tablespoons olive oil
1 tablespoon lemon juice
1 tablespoon chopped fresh coriander
$^1/_2$ Habanero or small red chilli, seeded and finely chopped

TO SERVE
6 flour tortillas
2 tablespoons olive oil
$^1/_2$ onion, sliced
$^1/_2$ Iceberg lettuce, roughly sliced
1 orange, peel and pith removed and thinly sliced
4 tablespoons Greek yoghurt

Pre-heat the oven to gas mark 6, 200°C, 400°F. Heat the oil in a frying-pan and add the onion. Cook for 3 minutes, or until softened. Then add three-quarters of the turkey mince, the cumin, flour, paprika, tomato purée, wine, stock and chilli and simmer for 8–10 minutes, or until the turkey is cooked and saucy. Add extra stock if necessary. Season with salt and pepper and keep warm.

Meanwhile, make the patties. Put the bread in a food processor and process for 10 seconds. Add the remaining turkey mince and process for 10 seconds. Add the coriander, half-chilli and egg yolk and process until mixed thoroughly. Mould the mixture into six small patties. Heat a frying-pan with the olive oil. Fry the patties for 3–5 minutes on each side, or until golden.

Place the tortillas on a baking sheet and bake for 3 minutes, to warm through.

Meanwhile, in a bowl mix the ingredients for the dressing. Keep to one side.

In a wok, heat the olive oil. Cut two of the tortillas into strips and, when the oil is smoking, stir-fry the tortilla strips and onion slices for about 2 minutes.

To assemble, put the lettuce and orange slices on a plate with the patties. Drizzle over the dressing and scatter the tortilla strips on top. On a separate plate, put a warmed tortilla. Spread on some of the turkey chilli and drizzle over the Greek yoghurt. Repeat with the remaining tortillas. Serve at once.

LESLEY WATERS

THAI-FRY

Stir-fried chicken noodles, served with chinese-leaf salad
with peanut sauce

Glenn from Rotherham told us there were two things he loved to do at the weekends:
one was cooking and the other was wallpapering his caravan! Fern and Lesley decided
to stick to cooking!

SERVES 2
FOR THE NOODLES

85 g (3oz) packet of instant rice noodles
1 boneless, skinless chicken breast, weighing
about 225 g (8 oz), sliced
1 tablespoon vegetable oil
1 fresh red chilli, seeded and
cut in small pieces
150 g (5 oz) beansprouts
2 spring onions, green tops only
Salt and freshly ground black pepper

FOR THE MARINADE

1 lime, cut in small pieces
1 teaspoon sesame oil
1 teaspoon soy sauce
2 tablespoons chopped fresh coriander
1 garlic clove, crushed

FOR THE OMELETTE

1 tablespoon sunflower oil
3 eggs
1 tablespoon chopped fresh coriander

FOR THE SALAD

1 small head of Chinese leaves, shredded
2 carrots, peeled into strips
2 teaspoons soy sauce
1 teaspoon sesame oil
Salt and freshly ground black pepper

FOR THE SAUCE

50 g (2 oz) unsalted skinned peanuts
1 tablespoon chopped fresh coriander
3 tablespoons water
1 teaspoon soy sauce
1 tablespoon Thai fish sauce, to taste
75 ml (3 fl oz) sunflower oil
Chopped fresh parsley
1 tablespoon lemon juice
Salt and freshly ground black pepper

TO SERVE

1 orange, peeled and sliced
2 spring onions, green tops only,
roughly chopped

Put the noodles in a large, deep pan or bowl, fill with boiling water and leave to soak for 6–10 minutes, or according to the packet instructions. Drain thoroughly.

Meanwhile, marinade the chicken in a bowl, with the lime pieces, sesame oil, soy sauce, coriander and garlic.

For the omelette, heat the oil in a non-stick fryng-pan. Lightly whisk the eggs in a bowl. Season and add the coriander. Pour into the frying-pan and make an omelette. To cook the other side, invert on to a plate and put back into the pan. Cook for 1–2 minutes. Tip on to a board, cool slightly, roll up and cut in strips.

In a bowl, put three-quarters of the Chinese leaves, the carrots, soy sauce and sesame oil. Toss together, season and leave to one side.

Now finish the noodles. Heat the oil in a wok and stir-fry the chicken with the marinade for 4–5 minutes, or until cooked. Add the reserved Chinese leaves, the chilli, beansprouts, half the green tops of the spring onions, the omelette and noodles. Season and toss together until heated through.

To make the peanut sauce, put three-quarters of the peanuts into a food processor, with the coriander, water, soy sauce and fish sauce. Process until smooth and, with the motor still running, slowly pour in the oil. Stir in some parsley and the lemon juice. Check and adjust the seasoning.

Serve the stir-fried noodles on a plate. Garnish with the remaining spring onions and reserved peanuts. Arrange the salad and the orange slices to the side and drizzle on some of the peanut sauce.

KEVIN WOODFORD

BOBBY'S BURGER SURPRISE

Turkey burgers with honey-roasted parsnips and kumquat marmalade

Bobby Hoyle wanted to surprise her dad with a special meal for Christmas. Much to his relief Kevin did most of the cooking as, since her seventh birthday, when he bought her a junior cookbook, she's been inflicting experiments – and disasters – from the kitchen on him.

SERVES 2

FOR THE PARSNIPS
1 tablespoon olive oil
15 g ($\frac{1}{2}$ oz) butter
1 tablespoon clear honey
8 baby parsnips, topped and tailed
1 tablespoon finely chopped fresh parsley
1 tablespoon finely chopped fresh coriander
Salt and freshly ground black pepper

FOR THE BURGERS
5 slices of white bread
Chopped fresh parsley
225 g (8 oz) turkey mince
2 rashers of bacon, chopped
2 garlic cloves, finely chopped
1 egg, beaten
Salt and freshly ground black pepper

TO COAT THE BURGERS
75 g (3 oz) plain flour
2 eggs, lightly beaten
1 tablespoon olive oil

FOR THE MARMALADE
40 g ($1\frac{1}{2}$ oz) butter
1 large onion, roughly chopped
1 garlic clove, finely chopped
150 g (5 oz) kumquats, sliced
2 tablespoons chopped fresh parsley
75 ml (3 fl oz) brandy
3 tablespoons cranberry sauce
Tabasco sauce

FOR THE CARROTS
6 baby carrots
Butter

TO GARNISH
Sage and dill sprigs

Pre-heat the oven to gas mark 6, 200°C, 400°F. Heat the oil and butter in an ovenproof pan, add the honey, toss in the parsnips and season, sprinkle the parsley and coriander on top, transfer to the oven and bake for 15–18 minutes.

Meanwhile, make the burgers. Put the bread in a food processor and blend into breadcrumbs. Add a handful of the parsley and blend in. Put the mince in a bowl, with the bacon and garlic, add the egg and a handful of breadcrumbs, mix together and season. Prepare a plate of seasoned flour, a plate of breadcrumbs and a shallow bowl of beaten egg. Take a ball of the turkey mince and coat it in flour, dip it in the egg and finally in the breadcrumbs. Flatten into a burger shape. Heat the oil in a frying-pan, put the burgers in and cook over a medium heat for about 5–6 minutes each side, or until cooked in the centre and golden brown.

For the hot marmalade, heat the butter in another frying-pan, add the onion and garlic and cook until softened. Add the kumquats and some parsley. Pour in the brandy and flambé, tilting and rotating the pan until the flames die down. Add the cranberry sauce and a couple of drops of Tabasco sauce and cook for a further 3–4 minutes.

Boil the carrots until tender. Drain, return to the pan and toss with a knob of butter, to glaze.

To serve, place the burgers on a plate, spoon the kumquat mixture on to the side, surround with the parsnips and carrots and garnish with dill and sage.

READY STEADY COOK Tips

Warm the brandy in the pan for a few seconds before you flambé it to enhance the flavour. If you are using gas, tilt the pan slightly to ignite the brandy. Otherwise use a taper. Let the alcohol burn off and the flames will then die down on their own.

Leave a little of the trimmed green stalks on the baby carrots for an attractive effect.

KEVIN WOODFORD

DISCIPLINED DUCK

Crisp-griddled duck with savoury rice, sweet and sour sauce, stir-fried vegetables and 'seaweed'

Working in a police complaints and discipline department, Jim Smith needed something special to impress 'the lads'.

SERVES 2

FOR THE RICE
25 g (1 oz) butter
1 garlic clove, crushed
4 spring onions, chopped
100 g (4 oz) long-grain rice
300 ml (10 fl oz) boiling water
2 eggs, beaten

FOR THE MARINADE
1 tablespoon white-wine vinegar
1 tablespoon honey
Tabasco sauce
juice of 1/2 orange
2 teaspoon chopped fresh coriander
1 garlic clove, crushed
2 boneless duck breasts
Salt and freshly ground black pepper

FOR THE SAUCE
4 teaspoons white-wine vinegar
2 tablespoons tomato ketchup
2 teaspoons brown sugar

FOR THE VEGETABLES
1 tablespoon vegetable oil
1 small onion, chopped
1 red pepper, seeded and sliced
1 courgette, thinly sliced

FOR THE 'SEAWEED'
6 tablespoons vegetable oil
250 g (9 oz) spring greens, finely shredded
Salt and freshly ground black pepper
Coriander leaves, to garnish

Pre-heat the oven to gas mark 7, 220°C, 425°F. Melt the butter in a pan and add the garlic, spring onions and rice. Cook together for 2 minutes before adding the water; reduce the heat and leave to simmer for 10–12 minutes, or until tender and most of the water has been absorbed. Add more water as necessary during cooking.

To make the marinade, in a bowl, mix together the vinegar, honey, a few drops of Tabasco sauce, the orange juice, coriander and garlic and season with salt and pepper. Add the duck and leave to marinate for a few minutes while you heat a griddle pan. Griddle the duck, skin-side down, for 4 minutes, until the skin is crisp. Transfer to the oven and continue cooking for 10–15 minutes.

Meanwhile, make the sauce. Into a small pan, put the vinegar, tomato ketchup and sugar and simmer together for 1–2 minutes, adding a little water to make a smooth sauce.

For the stir-fried vegetables, heat the oil and stir-fry the onion, pepper and courgette for 2–3 minutes.

For the 'seaweed', heat the remaining oil in a wok and stir-fry the shredded spring greens for 4–5 minutes, until crisp but still green and season. Drain on kitchen paper.

Stir the eggs into the rice and heat through. Do not overheat as the mixture will curdle. To serve, carve the duck into slices. Put a bed of rice on two warmed serving plates. Spoon the stir-fried vegetables on to the rice and arrange the slices of duck and 'seaweed' on top. Keep warm. Pour the duck cooking juices into the sauce and heat through. Then pour the sauce round the rice and garnish the dish with coriander leaves.

KEVIN WOODFORD

NAN'S CELEBRATION RABBIT

Rabbit casserole with herby dumplings and orange leeks

Nan Bourne was invited along to our VE Day show as she had been in the fire service during the war, driving mobile canteens and manning the pumps. A further cause for celebration was the fact that her 55th wedding anniversary was just two weeks away.

SERVES 2	1 rabbit, cut into chunks and small sharp
FOR THE CASSEROLE	bones removed
2 tablespoons sunflower oil	2 carrots, sliced

1 tablespoon chopped fresh parsley
1 tablespoon chopped fresh coriander
1 tablespoon chopped fresh mint
1 tablespoon plain flour
1 tablespoon tomato purée
300 ml (10 fl oz) red wine
1 potato, peeled and cut into balls *à la Parisienne* or chopped
Salt and freshly ground black pepper

FOR THE LEEKS
3 leeks, cut in 1 cm (½ in) slices

25 g (1 oz) butter
Juice of 1 orange
Salt and freshly ground black pepper

FOR THE DUMPLINGS
50 g (2 oz) self-raising flour
25 g (1 oz) vegetable suet
1 tablespoon chopped fresh parsley
2 tablespoons chopped fresh coriander
1 tablespoon chopped fresh mint
2 tablespoons water
Salt and freshly ground black pepper

To make the rabbit casserole, heat the oil in heavy-based frying-pan and brown the rabbit pieces, carrots and parsley, coriander and mint. Stir in the flour and tomato purée and cook for a further minute. Then pour in the wine, stirring continuously, and bring to the boil. The sauce should thicken. Add the potato balls and let the rabbit simmer for 12–15 minutes, until the rabbit is cooked (the juices should run clear). Season to taste.

Sauté the leeks in the butter for 4 minutes, stirring occasionally. Add the orange juice, season and cook for a further 2–3 minutes.

For the dumplings, mix the flour, suet and seasoning with the herbs and water, to form a sticky mixture. Shape into little balls and cook in a pan of simmering water for 5 minutes.

To serve, spoon the rabbit casserole on to two warmed plates and arrange the dumplings around the edge. Serve the leeks separately.

READY STEADY COOK Tip
If you don't like rabbit, try this idea with chicken portions. They will need to be cooked in the casserole for at least 30 minutes, depending on size. Check that they are cooked through, by piercing the thickest part with a skewer; the juices should be clear, not pink, and the flesh should be white.

KEVIN WOODFORD

HEAVEN ON EARTH

Chicken breast stuffed with apricots, pepper and chicory salad, spicy rice and cucumber salad

Rita Chada from Birmingham named her dish Heaven on Earth, not only because it tasted delicious but also because cooking without her 'clumsy and useless in the kitchen' husband certainly did feel like heaven!

SERVES 2

FOR THE RICE
100 g (4 oz) long-grain rice
1 garlic clove, crushed
2 teaspoons garam masala

FOR THE CHICKEN
1 shallot, chopped
1 button mushroom, sliced
$^1/_2$ small red pepper, seeded and chopped
25 g (1 oz) butter
6 canned apricot halves in natural juice, sliced
2 boneless, skinless chicken breasts
1 chicken stock cube, dissolved in

600 ml (1 pint) boiling water
Salt and freshly ground black pepper

FOR THE CUCUMBER SALAD
2 tablespoons Greek yoghurt
$^1/_2$ cucumber, sliced
2 tablespoons chopped fresh mint

FOR THE SALAD
1 small oak-leaf lettuce
$^1/_2$ red pepper, seeded and chopped
1 head of chicory
2 teaspoons medium curry powder
125 ml (4 fl oz) good-quality mayonnaise
Salt and freshly ground black pepper

Pre-heat the oven to gas mark 7, 220°C, 425°F. Cook the rice in salted, boiling water, with the crushed garlic and the garam masala, according to the instructions on the packet.

Sauté the shallot, mushroom and red pepper in the butter for 5 minutes and season. Add the apricots and continue cooking for 2 minutes. Flatten each chicken breast with a rolling-pin between two sheets of cling film to a thickness of 5 mm (¼ in). Spoon half the mushroom and pepper mixture on to each chicken breast. Roll up each breast and lightly wrap each one in foil. Put the rolled chicken in an ovenproof dish, with the stock and cook for 15 minutes, until the chicken is cooked and no longer pink. Unwrap, allow the rolls to cool slightly and carefully slice each breast into four or five.

To make the cucumber salad, mix the yoghurt with the cucumber and mint.

For the salad, arrange the lettuce, red pepper and chicory leaves on each plate. Mix the curry powder into the mayonnaise and, if necessary, thin it slightly with a tablespoon of water and season.

To serve, arrange the chicken slices on a bed of the rice and spoon the mayonnaise over the chicken. Serve on the same plate as the cucumber and salad.

K E V I N   W O O D F O R D

BURFORD QUAIL

Casseroled quail in red wine, with shredded sprouts and sweet-potato mash

Wendy fancied challenging Kevin to something a bit unusual and tipped a quail from her bag, grinning from ear to ear. She told us that she was always happy 'which annoys my grumpy husband intensely'.

SERVES 2

FOR THE CASSEROLE
2 tablespoons oil
1 onion, roughly chopped
3 celery sticks, roughly chopped
1 leek, sliced
2 quails
450 ml (15 fl oz) red wine

FOR THE SWEET-POTATO MASH
450 g (1 lb) sweet potato, peeled and cubed

15 g (½ oz) butter
Salt and freshly ground black pepper

FOR THE BRUSSELS SPROUTS
350 g (12 oz) Brussels sprouts
1 tablespoon olive oil
Salt and freshly ground black pepper

FOR THE BEURRE MANIÉ
15 g (½ oz) butter, softened
15 g (½ oz) plain flour

Heat the oil in a pan, add the onion, celery and leek and cook until softened. Add the quail and seal until well browned. Pour in the wine, making sure the liquid covers the quail. Cover with a lid and simmer at just below boiling point for 15 minutes, turning the quail halfway through cooking.

Meanwhile, boil the sweet-potatoes in salted water for 10 minutes. Drain and add a knob of butter. Season with salt and pepper and then mash well.

Peel the outer layer from the sprouts, cut off the stems and grate the remainder. Heat the oil in a frying-pan, add the sprouts, season and fry gently for 3–4 minutes, until slightly softened.

Make the *beurre manié* by kneading the butter in a bowl with your fingers and working in the flour. Remove the quail from the pan and keep warm. Stir the *beurre manié* a little at a time into the red wine stock, to thicken it.

Arrange the vegetables on two warmed plates, put the quails on top and pour over the thickened red-wine sauce.

READY STEADY COOK Tips

Beurre manié *means 'kneaded butter'. It is a good way to thicken all kinds of sauces and casseroles at the end of cooking, giving a rich and shiny appearance.*

If you don't want to use quail or another kind of game bird in this recipe, try it with a small chicken or poussin, halved, or chicken portions.

KEVIN WOODFORD

POSTMASTER PETE'S DUCKLING

Golden duck legs with parsnip sauce, saffron rice and sesame broccoli

Peter Dimaline, from Doncaster, claimed that he'd 'kill for duck' and wanted a dish that included masses of ginger; he's generally deprived of his favourite flavouring, because his wife hates it!

SERVES 2

FOR THE DUCK

2 x 225 g (8 oz) duckling legs, boned
2 parsley sprigs
2 teaspoons wholegrain mustard
1 tablespoon sunflower oil
Salt and freshly ground black pepper

FOR THE SAUCE

225 g (8 oz) parsnips, cut in 2 cm ($^3/_4$ in) cubes
1 teaspoon mustard
2 teaspoons clear honey
1 cm ($^1/_2$ in) piece of fresh root ginger, peeled and finely chopped
1 tablespoon chopped fresh parsley
Juice of 2 limes
150 ml (5 fl oz) red wine
Salt and freshly ground black pepper

FOR THE RICE

1 tablespoon sunflower oil
2 shallots or 1 small onion, finely chopped
100 g (4 oz) long-grain rice
Pinch of saffron threads
450 ml (15 fl oz) water
Salt and freshly ground black pepper

FOR THE BROCCOLI

1 tablespoon sunflower oil
225 g (8 oz) broccoli, cut in small florets
2 garlic cloves, crushed
1 tablespoon sesame seeds
15 g ($^1/_2$ oz) butter
Salt and freshly ground black pepper

TO GARNISH

Slices of lime
Flatleaf parsley sprigs

Pre-heat the oven to gas mark 6, 200°C, 400°F. Season the duckling legs, put a sprig of parsley in the centre of each and then roll up and secure with kitchen string. Spread a teaspoon of mustard over each duckling roll. Heat the oil in a frying-pan and fry the duckling for 5 minutes, turning until golden. Transfer to a baking tray and bake for 12–15 minutes.

Meanwhile, cook the parsnips in a pan of salted, boiling water for 8–10 minutes until tender.

For the rice, heat the oil in a pan, add the shallots or onion and cook for a minute. Stir in the rice, saffron and seasoning and then add the water. Bring to the boil and cook for 8–10 minutes, until the rice is tender.

Drain and mash the parsnips. Stir in the mustard, honey, ginger, parsley, lime juice, wine and seasoning. Simmer for 5 minutes, until the sauce has reduced slightly.

Heat the oil in a frying-pan, add the broccoli, garlic and sesame seeds and season with salt and pepper. Stir-fry for 2 minutes. Stir in the butter and cook for a minute.

Spoon the rice into two 10 cm (4 in) ramekin dishes and press down lightly.

To serve, turn the rice out on to two warmed serving plates. Arrange a duckling leg next to the rice. Spoon over the parsnip sauce and garnish with slices of lime and sprigs of flatleaf parsley. Serve with the sesame broccoli.

READY STEADY COOK Tips

Flatleaf parsley has a fuller flavour than the more common curled parsley, although this is fine to use instead if you do not have the continental variety.

Cut the broccoli in even-sized florets so that they all cook in the same amount of time to a tender but slightly crisp finish.

Freshly squeezed lime juice is the best thing to use, but you can now buy bottled lime juice, which is handy to have in the fridge to pep up your cooking.

MEAT DISHES

LESLEY WATERS

PIG OUT

Sliced white hog's pudding, with warm potato salad and sweet and sour red cabbage

Never having tried white hog's pudding before, Jim Cribbett was more than happy to 'pig out' on this hearty meal.

SERVES 2–4

FOR THE POTATOES
100 g (4 oz) new potatoes, halved lengthways
2 tablespoons olive oil

FOR THE CABBAGE
2 tablespoons olive oil
1 baby red cabbage, sliced
150 ml (5 fl oz) red wine
1½ tablespoons caster sugar
1 teaspoon red-wine vinegar
225 g (8 oz) spring greens, shredded
150 g (5 oz) pancetta, cubed

FOR THE PUDDING
2 tablespoons olive oil
225 g (8 oz) white hog's pudding, or black pudding, sliced thickly
1 red onion, sliced
1 green apple, cored and sliced

FOR THE DRESSING
1 tablespoon balsamic vinegar
1 tablespoon olive oil
1 tablespoon chopped fresh rosemary
Salt and freshly ground black pepper

Cook the potatoes in boiling, salted water, until tender.

Heat the oil in a frying-pan and cook the red cabbage for 4 minutes. Add the wine, sugar and vinegar and continue cooking for a further 4 minutes until just tender.

Blanch the spring greens in boiling, salted water for a minute. Refresh under cold water and set to one side.

Add the cubed pancetta to the cabbage and season with salt and ground black pepper.

Heat the oil in a frying-pan and fry the hog's pudding slices for 2 minutes on each side. Add the onion and apple and cook for 3–4 minutes or until golden.

Heat another pan with the 2 tablespoons of oil. Add the potatoes and fry until golden and crisp.

Mix together the dressing ingredients, season and pour over the potatoes.

Heat a little oil in a wok and tip in the greens, just to warm through.

Divide the cabbage and greens between warmed serving plates. Arrange the hog's pudding slices around the outside, with the apples and onions and the potatoes.

LESLEY WATERS

CAROLE'S KEBABS

Minced lamb kebabs with vegetables in wine, spinach and orange salad and creamed spinach

Carole came on the show with a mission. 'Please show me something interesting to do with mince', she begged. Lesley obliged with these Middle-Eastern-style minced-meat kebabs.

SERVES 2

FOR THE KEBABS
450 g (1 lb) minced lamb or beef
1 tablespoon ground cumin
1 tablespoon ground coriander
2 teaspoons dried oregano
1 egg white
1 tablespoon olive oil
Salt and freshly ground black pepper

FOR THE VEGETABLES
2 tablespoon olive oil
1 onion, sliced
1 fennel bulb, cut in 5 cm (2 in) pieces
1 red pepper, seeded and sliced
1 medium potato, halved and thinly sliced
100 ml (4 fl oz) white wine

FOR THE CITRUS DRESSING
Juice of 1 lemon
2 oranges
3 tablespoons olive oil
Salt and freshly ground black pepper

FOR THE SPINACH
225 g (8 oz) fresh spinach, washed
2 tablespoons double cream
Pinch of grated nutmeg
Salt and freshly ground black pepper
2 tablespoons chopped fresh coriander, to garnish

Pre-heat the oven to gas mark 8, 230°C, 450°F or pre-heat the grill to hot. Put the lamb, cumin, coriander, oregano and egg white in a bowl. Season with salt and pepper and mix thoroughly with your hands. Divide the mixture into four and shape into sausages around oiled kebab skewers. Wrap the ends of the skewers in foil, put them on a baking tray and drizzle the oil over the kebabs. Cook for 10–12 minutes, until the vegetables are tender, turning occasionally.

For the vegetables, heat the oil in a pan and cook the onion for 5 minutes. Add the fennel, pepper and potato and cook for 8–10 minutes. Add the wine and cook for 3–4 minutes.

Put the lemon juice and juice of one orange in a bowl with the oil and season with salt and pepper. Cut all the peel and white pith off the second orange and slice it thinly. Toss half the spinach, the orange slices and half of the citrus dressing together.

Put the remaining spinach in a pan, with just the water that clings to its leaves, and cook for 2 minutes, until wilted. Stir in the cream, nutmeg and seasoning and cook for a minute.

To serve, put the mixed vegetables on two warmed plates and drizzle over the rest of the citrus dressing. Remove the foil and put the kebabs on top, sprinkle over the chopped coriander. Serve with the creamed spinach and the spinach and orange salad.

LESLEY WATERS

GOULASH AND MASH

Beef goulash with mashed potatoes and spiced fried bread

With winter approaching thick and fast, Alistair Burns wanted a heartwarming dish to see him through the cold months.

SERVES 2	15 g (¹/₂ oz) butter
FOR THE MASH	3 tablespoons milk
450 g (1 lb) potatoes, cut in	225 g (8 oz) Greek yoghurt
1 cm (¹/₂ in) cubes	

MEAT DISHES

2 tablespoons roughly chopped fresh parsley

Salt and freshly ground black pepper

FOR THE GOULASH

2 tablespoons olive oil

1 large onion, chopped

Pinch of sugar

1 green pepper, seeded and chopped

1 red pepper, seeded and chopped

2 tablespoons paprika

350 g (12 oz) stir-fry beef strips

Cayenne pepper

150 ml (5 fl oz) red wine

450 g (1 lb) tomatoes, roughly chopped

1 tablespoon lemon juice

1 bay leaf

150 ml (5 fl oz) vegetable or beef stock

FOR THE SPICED BREAD

50 g (2 oz) butter

1 tablespoon sunflower oil

1 teaspoon ground cumin

1 teaspoon paprika

2 thick slices of bread, cut in rough chunks

Cook the potatoes in a pan of salted, boiling water for 8–10 minutes, until tender.

Meanwhile, for the goulash, heat the oil in a large pan, add the onion and cook for 3 minutes. Add the green and red peppers and cook for 2 minutes. Stir in the paprika and cook for a minute more. Add the beef and a pinch of Cayenne pepper and season with salt, pepper and the sugar. Cook, stirring, for 2 minutes. Add the wine, tomatoes, lemon juice and bay leaf and simmer for 10 minutes, adding 3–4 tablespoons of stock if the sauce gets too thick. Remove the bay leaf.

Heat the butter and oil in a large frying-pan, add the cumin and paprika and cook for 30 seconds. Fry the bread in the spiced butter for 3–4 minutes, turning once and taking care not to burn the spices.

Drain the potatoes, add the butter and mash well. Mix in the milk, 4 tablespoons of the yoghurt, the parsley and seasoning.

Thin the rest of the yoghurt with 1–2 tablespoons of water. To serve, spoon the goulash on to a plate and serve with the mashed potatoes and spiced fried bread. Serve the yoghurt separately.

LESLEY WATERS

MOUTHWATERING MEDITERRANEAN MAGIC

Marinated lamb chops with garlic-mashed potatoes, ratatouille and aubergine

School teacher, Paul Caine, loves to get his pupils cooking and had recently turned the classroom into a French bistro. His pupils got revenge by sending him to the programme.

SERVES 2

FOR THE LAMB
1 lamb steak, halved, or 2 chump chops
1 tablespoon white wine
1 tablespoon olive oil
5–6 sage leaves, shredded
Salt and freshly ground black pepper

FOR THE RATATOUILLE
2 tablespoons olive oil
1 onion, chopped
1 garlic clove, roughly chopped
4 apricots, stoned and quartered
3 tablespoons white wine
5 tomatoes, roughly chopped
1 tablespoon tomato purée

10 pitted green olives, halved
Salt and freshly ground black pepper

FOR THE MASHED POTATOES
350 g (12 oz) potatoes, peeled and cubed
1 garlic clove, crushed
2 tablespoons basil, roughly chopped
2 tablespoons double cream
2 tablespoons milk
Salt and freshly ground black pepper

FOR THE AUBERGINE
1 aubergine, sliced thickly
Juice of 1 lemon
7 tablespoons olive oil
Salt and freshly ground black pepper

Marinate the lamb in the wine, oil, sage and salt and pepper for at least 10 minutes (if time, for 1–2 hours).

To make the ratatouille, heat the oil and sweat the onion for a few minutes, until it is soft and translucent. Add the garlic and sauté for a minute. Then add the apricots and continue to cook for 3–4 minutes. Stir in the wine, tomatoes, and tomato purée, season with salt and black pepper and simmer for 10 minutes. Then stir in the olives.

For the mashed potatoes, boil the potatoes in salted, boiling water for 12–15 minutes. Drain and mash the potatoes with the garlic, basil, cream and milk. Season. For a milder taste, fry the garlic for 30 seconds in a little oil and butter, before adding it to the potatoes.

Pre-heat the barbecue or grill. Soak the aubergine slices for 5 minutes in the lemon juice, salt and pepper and 5 tablespoons of the oil. Then fry the aubergine with the marinade in the remaining 2 tablespoons of oil for 5 minutes. Grill the lamb for 5–6 minutes on each side.

To serve, put the aubergines on warmed plates. Arrange the lamb on top, with the ratatouille on the side and serve with the potatoes.

KEVIN WOODFORD

AUBERGINE MAGGLIACCIO

Aubergines stuffed with creamy pork, with saffron rice

Pauline was married to an Italian whose mother was a fantastic cook, so she was desperate for Kevin to give her some tips to impress her man with

SERVES 2

FOR THE AUBERGINES
25 g (1 oz) butter
1 tablespoon oil
225 g (8 oz) pork fillet, trimmed and cut in
1 cm ($\frac{1}{2}$ in) cubes
1 aubergine
3 spring onions, chopped
1 dessert apple, peeled, cored and chopped
1 tablespoon snipped fresh chives
1 tablespoon chopped fresh coriander
1 tablespoon chopped fresh parsley
2 tablespoons Dijon mustard

90 ml (3 fl oz) white wine
2 tablespoons double cream
2 tablespoons grated parmesan cheese
Salt and freshly ground black pepper

FOR THE RICE
1 tablespoon oil
2 spring onions, chopped
1 garlic clove, crushed
100 g (4 oz) long-grain rice
Pinch of saffron threads
$\frac{1}{2}$ chicken stock cube, dissolved in 300 ml
(10 fl oz) boiling water

Heat the butter and oil in a frying-pan and fry the pork for 2 minutes. Cut the aubergine in half lengthways, spoon out the flesh and chop it. Keep the shells. Add the aubergine flesh, spring onions, apple and herbs to the frying-pan and season with salt and pepper. Continue cooking for 3 minutes. Stir in the mustard and wine and bring to the boil. Turn down the heat and simmer until the pork is almost cooked. Mix in the cream and parmesan cheese and continue to cook until the sauce has thickened. Meanwhile, pre-heat the grill to hot.

Pile the pork mixture into the aubergine skins and place under the pre-heated grill for 8 minutes.

Meanwhile, make the rice. Sauté the spring onions in the oil until softened. Add the garlic and rice and sauté for 1–2 minutes, until the rice grains are well coated in oil. Stir in the saffron and the stock. Reduce the heat and cook until the rice has absorbed the liquid. When the rice is cooked, spoon it into two ramekins.

To serve, put the stuffed aubergine halves on two warmed plates. Turn out the rice so it forms a small, neat mound next to the aubergine.

LESLEY WATERS

TONE'S POT BELLY PORK

Marinated belly pork with spiced red cabbage with apple and garlic roast potatoes

Tone from Staffordshire had but one plea for Lesley: 'Can you give my red cabbage some "oomph"?' This spicy cabbage mixture is slightly sweet and sour and packs a real flavour punch, enough to make it a robust partner for garlicky potatoes and marinated belly of pork.

SERVES 2	2 teaspoons tomato purée
FOR THE MARINADE	A few drops of Tabasco sauce
2 teaspoons Worcestershire sauce	1 teaspoon dried mixed herbs
4 teaspoons soy sauce	3 teaspoons wholegrain mustard
2 ½ tablespoons clear honey	Sprig of fresh rosemary

FOR THE PORK
300 g (11 oz) belly pork, cut in two
1 tablespoon olive oil
2 tablespoons red wine

FOR THE POTATOES
2 medium potatoes
Olive oil
1 clove garlic, chopped

FOR THE CABBAGE
1 tablespoon olive oil
1 onion, cut in large chunks

1 cooking apple, peeled, cored, halved and sliced
1 green pepper, seeded and sliced
1 red cabbage, shredded
1 teaspoon balsamic vinegar
100 ml (3½ fl oz) red wine
25 g (1 oz) butter
2 star-anise
1 tablespoon fresh chopped chervil
1 teaspoon caster sugar
Salt and freshly ground black pepper
1 tablespoon Greek yoghurt, to serve
Chervil sprigs, to garnish

Pre-heat the oven to gas mark 7, 220°C, 425°F. In a bowl, mix together the marinade ingredients. De-rind and trim the pork pieces and put them in the bowl. Leave to one side.

Cut the potatoes in half and cut as for fantail potatoes. Par-boil in salted, boiling water for 3 minutes. Drain and brush generously with olive oil. Place in an ovenproof dish, with the garlic. Put in the oven and bake for 20 minutes, until they are cooked through, crisp and golden.

For the cabbage, heat the oil in a wok or deep frying-pan. Fry the onion for 3 minutes or until soft. Add the apple and most of the pepper and cook for a further 5 minutes. Add the cabbage, vinegar, wine, butter, star-anise, chervil and sugar. Season with salt and pepper. Stir continuously for a minute. Cover and leave over a gentle heat for 5 minutes.

Fry the pork with the rest of the pepper in the oil and the marinade in a frying-pan for 8 minutes, turning occasionally. Remove from the pan and deglaze the pan with the wine.

To serve, divide the cabbage between two warmed plates and top with a little Greek yoghurt. Set the pork pieces to one side of the cabbage and pour the sauce over each. Garnish with chervil. Serve with the potatoes.

K E V I N   W O O D F O R D

BEST OF BEEF BAKE

Beef in puff-pastry parcels, with béarnaise sauce and
patty-pan squashes

Being a national champion at tug-of-war, Angie Benson wanted Kevin to cook up a hearty beef dish that she could serve to her team-mates.

SERVES 2

FOR THE STEAKS
100 g (4 oz) chicken livers
2 shallots, roughly chopped
1 tablespoon chopped fresh parsley
4 button mushrooms, roughly chopped
1 plum tomato, skinned and chopped
1 garlic clove
Brandy
2 tablespoons olive oil
2 x 125 g (4 oz) ready-rolled
puff pastry sheets
2 x 150–175 g (5–6 oz) fillet steaks
1 tablespoon mustard
1 egg yolk, beaten
Salt and freshly ground black pepper

FOR THE SAUCE
2 egg yolks
1 tablespoon white wine
75 g (3 oz) unsalted butter, melted
1 tablespoon chopped fresh parsley
1 tablespoon chopped fresh coriander

FOR THE SQUASHES
25 g (1 oz) butter
6 button mushrooms
2 small squashes, quartered and seeded
Salt and freshly ground black pepper

TO SERVE
1 plum tomato, chopped
Dill sprigs

Pre-heat the oven to gas mark 7, 220°C, 425°F. Put the chicken livers, shallots, parsley, mushrooms, tomato, garlic and a splash of brandy into a food processor, season and blend until quite smooth. Transfer the mixture to a hot frying-pan and fry in 1 tablespoon of the oil.

Roll out each piece of pastry into a 20 cm (8 in) square. Flatten the steaks to 5 cm (2 in) thick, by beating them with a rolling-pin or meat hammer. Heat the remaining oil in a hot frying-pan and seal the steaks for a minute on each side. Place the steaks in the middle of the pastry and brush them with mustard. Spoon the chicken-liver mixture on top. Brush the edges of the pastry with beaten egg yolk and fold the pastry to enclose the meat. Brush the pastry with beaten egg yolk, to glaze. Bake for 15 minutes or until the pastry has browned.

To make the béarnaise sauce, whisk the egg yolks in a heatproof bowl over a pan of simmering water (the water must not touch the bottom of the bowl). Add the wine and whisk until the mixture thickens and the whisk leaves a trail. Gradually stir in the melted butter, leaving the sediment behind in the pan, and, finally, the parsley and coriander.

Meanwhile, heat the butter in a frying-pan, add the whole mushrooms and squashes. Season and fry for 4–5 minutes.

To serve, put the pastry parcels on warmed plates and garnish with chopped tomato and dill sprigs. Spoon some sauce on the side and accompany with the squashes and mushrooms.

K E V I N W O O D F O R D

BONFIRE BONANZA BROTH

Bacon 'Catherine wheels' and bacon and sweetcorn soup

For Bonfire Night, Rachel wanted something to impress her husband, who, she admitted, was the better cook 'which can be incredibly annoying at times', she added.

SERVES 4

FOR THE CATHERINE WHEELS
150 g (5 oz) shortcrust pastry
1 egg, beaten
225 g (8 oz) unsmoked streaky bacon

FOR THE SOUP
50 g (2 oz) butter
1 onion, chopped
2 garlic cloves, crushed
1 vegetable stock cube, dissolved in 900 ml

(1½ pints) boiling water
2 corn on the cob or 100 g (4 oz) tinned or frozen sweetcorn kernels, drained
1 red pepper, seeded and chopped
2 turnips, peeled and chopped
225 g (8 oz) smoked pork sausage, sliced
275 g (10 oz) potatoes, peeled and cubed
1 tablespoon tomato purée
2 tablespoons chopped fresh coriander
Salt and freshly ground black pepper

VARIATION   Worcestershire sauce
Tabasco sauce   1–2 garlic cloves, crushed
$1/2$ teaspoon chilli powder

Pre-heat the oven to gas mark 6, 200°C, 400°F. Roll out the pastry on a floured board into a 25 cm (10 in) by 13 cm (5 in) oblong about 5 mm ($1/4$ in) thick and brush with some of the egg. De-rind five rashers of the bacon and lay them on top of the pastry. Roll the pastry into a sausage lengthways, cut it into 1 cm ($1/2$ in) slices and brush with the remaining egg. Put on a greased baking sheet and bake for 12–15 minutes, or until golden.

For the soup, melt the butter in a saucepan, add the onion and garlic and cook until soft. Add the stock. Cut the remaining bacon into strips. Cut the kernels from the corn cobs, if using. Add the bacon and corn to the soup, with the red pepper, turnips, sausage, potatoes, tomato purée, coriander and seasoning. Bring to the boil, then simmer for 15–20 minutes, until potatoes are tender.

For a spicier version, add 3 drops of Tabasco, the chilli powder, a splash of Worcestershire sauce and some extra garlic into the pan with the stock and continue recipe as above.

MEAT DISHES

KEVIN WOODFORD

ANNETTE'S AUSSIE ARTICHOKES

Marinated pork medallions with artichoke crisps and soubise sauce

Having returned to Banstead from Australia, Annette Richardson was keen to combine true British cooking with a bit of down under. The finished meal was so delicious, Annette was tempted to stay.

SERVES 2

FOR THE RICE
1 tablespoon olive oil
1/2 onion, chopped
100 g (4 oz) rice
1 garlic clove, crushed
1 tablespoon chopped fresh coriander
1 tablespoon chopped fresh parsley
1 tablespoon chopped fresh dill
400 ml (14 fl oz) chicken stock

FOR THE ARTICHOKE CRISPS
1 tablespoon lemon juice
2 Jerusalem artichokes, peeled
Oil for deep-frying

FOR THE MEDALLIONS
2 tablespoons clear honey
1 tablespoon Dijon mustard

4 tablespoons olive oil
2 parsley sprigs
2 pork chops
Salt and freshly ground black pepper

FOR THE VEGETABLES
1/2 onion, chopped
1 yellow pepper, sliced
50 g (2 oz) mushrooms, sliced
2 tablespoons white wine

FOR THE SAUCE
2 tablespoon double cream
1 egg yolk
Parsley sprigs, to garnish

For the rice, heat the oil in a pan, add the onion and cook for 3 minutes. Add the rice, garlic, herbs and stock. Bring the mixture to the boil and reduce the heat and then cover. Cook thoroughly for 12–15 minutes, until the rice is tender and has absorbed all the liquid.

Add the lemon juice to a bowl of cold water and put in the artichoke slices as you cut them thinly, using a mandolin or sharp knife.

To make the marinade, put the honey, mustard, 2 tablespoons of oil, parsley and seasoning into a bowl and mix well. Trim the bone and fat off the chops to leave the medallion, place the meat in the marinade, turn to coat both sides and leave for at least 5 minutes.

Heat the remaining oil in a pan, add the pork and cook on both sides for 2 minutes. Transfer to grill pan and grill for 4 minutes on each side, until thoroughly cooked.

Add the onion, pepper and mushrooms to the pan in which you cooked the pork and cook for 2 minutes. Add the wine and cook until tender.

To fry the crisps, heat the oil for deep-frying in a wok or deep frying-pan. Drain the artichoke slices and pat dry on kitchen paper. Add them to the hot oil, in batches, if necessary, and cook until crisp and lightly browned. Drain on kitchen paper.

For the sauce, whip the cream until thick and add the egg yolk. Place in a food processor, with 3 tablespoons of the rice and blend together, until smooth.

Divide the remaining rice between two warmed plates. Add the pork, with a spoonful of the soubise sauce on top. Put the pepper and mushroom mixture round the side and garnish with the artichoke crisps and sprigs of parsley.

READY STEADY COOK Tips
Always drop artichoke slices into acidulated water to prevent them from turning brown.

If you can leave the meat in the marinade a little longer, it will help to improve the flavours.

You can make 'crisps' with other vegetables such as aubergine, courgette – or potato!

DESSERTS

L E S L E Y   W A T E R S

DIVERTING DESSERT SELECTION

Cherry and chocolate baked Alaska, caramelized satsumas and hot cherry sauce and vanilla ice cream

Jan Cooper brought along things she always has hanging around her house at Christmas and wondered if something exciting could come from after-dinner mints and satsumas: it could!

SERVES 10	25 cm (10 in) sponge flan case
FOR THE SATSUMAS	680 g (1 lb 6 oz) jar of pitted cherries in syrup
100 g (4 oz) granulated sugar	2 litres (3½ pints) vanilla ice cream
10 satsumas	100 g (4 oz) chocolate mint wafers
Juice of 1 orange	2 teaspoons arrowroot
100 ml (3½ fl oz) water	2 tablespoons cold water

FOR THE ALASKA AND HOT CHERRIES	**TO DECORATE**
5 size-3 egg whites	Icing sugar
375 g (13 oz) caster sugar	Mint sprigs

Pre-heat the oven to gas mark 7, 220°C, 425°F. Put the granulated sugar in a heavy-based pan with half the water. Heat gently until the sugar has dissolved. Boil steadily, without stirring, for 10–12 minutes, until the syrup turns to caramel and is golden brown. Add the remaining water (take care to stand back as the pan will hiss). Stir until all the lumps have dissolved and set to one side.

Put the unpeeled satsumas in a bowl, cover with boiling water and set aside.

Whisk the egg whites to stiff peaks and then gradually whisk in 275 g (10 oz) of the caster sugar. Continue whisking until the meringue mixture is very thick and glossy.

Put the flan case on a baking sheet and spoon half of the cherries into the case. Pile half of the ice cream on top of the cherries and soften slightly with a spoon. Break the chocolate mints into pieces and push them into the ice cream. Spread the meringue mixture all over the ice cream, making sure there are no gaps, and then sprinkle over 25 g (1 oz) of caster sugar. Bake for 4–5 minutes, until the meringue is lightly browned. Don't allow it to burn. Dust the baked Alaska with icing sugar and decorate with sprigs of mint.

Put the rest of the cherries, the syrup from the jar and the remaining sugar in a pan. Blend the arrowroot with the water and stir into the cherries and syrup. Bring to the boil, stirring all the time, until thickened.

Drain the satsumas, peel and put in a serving bowl. Add the orange juice to the caramel and pour over the satsumas. Stir well, to coat them in the caramel. Spoon the remaining ice cream into serving bowls and spoon over the hot cherry sauce. Serve the desserts.

L E S L E Y   W A T E R S

KELLY'S SUMMER COLLECTION

Cinnamon meringues, poached peaches, chocolate-dipped brazil nuts and raspberry purée

Kelly Holmes' husband dominated the barbecue over the summer. Kelly had resigned herself just to making the dessert and was looking for something a bit different to steal some of the limelight for herself.

SERVES 2

FOR THE MERINGUES
2 egg whites
100 g (4 oz) caster sugar
2 teaspoons ground cinnamon

FOR THE CHOCOLATE NUTS
75 g (3 oz) whole brazil nuts
50 g (2 oz) plain chocolate chips

FOR THE POACHED PEACHES
150 g (5 oz) caster sugar
3 tablespoons white wine
4 tablespoons water
Juice of 2 oranges
4 cloves
2 peaches, halved and stoned
15 g (½ oz) butter

FOR THE RASPBERRY PURÉE
100 g (4 oz) frozen raspberries
Icing sugar

Mint sprig, to garnish
200 ml (7 floz) ¹/₂ x carton crème fraîche

Pre-heat the oven to gas mark 5, 190°C, 375°F. Whisk the egg whites until they hold their shape. While still whisking, add 100 g (4 oz) of the caster sugar, a tablespoon at a time, until the meringue is stiff and shiny. Fold in the cinnamon. Shape the meringues into nine quenelles (egg shapes), using two spoons. Put the quenelles on to baking parchment on a baking sheet and bake for 6–7 minutes, until nicely coloured but still soft in the middle.

Lightly toast the nuts on a baking sheet in the oven for 4–5 minutes as well, turning occasionally.

Melt the chocolate chips in a double boiler and, when melted, dip the whole toasted brazil nuts in it, so that half is covered with the chocolate. Leave to set on baking parchment. With a piping bag drizzle the remaining chocolate over the mergingues.

In a small saucepan, put the remaining sugar, the wine and 2 tablespoons of the water and allow the sugar to dissolve.

Add half the orange juice to the sugar syrup, with another 2 tablespoons of water and the cloves. Put the peaches in, flesh-side down, and leave to poach for 8–10 minutes, until softened but still firm in the centre.

Put the frozen raspberries and a tablespoon of icing sugar into a food processor and process to make a purée.

Flood each plate with the raspberry purée. Place a poached peach in the centre of each plate and decorate with the chocolate covered nuts and meringues. Garnish with a sprig of mint and serve with the créme fraîche in a separate dish.

D E S S E R T S

L E S L E Y   W A T E R S

PUT-YOUR-FEET-UP PUDDING

Individual ratafia trifles, ratafia and nectarine *brûlée* and strawberries and cream swirl

At six feet six inches, Matthew Rose towered above Lesley and Fern as he tipped his ingredients on to the counter. It was only a couple of days away from Mother's Day and Matthew wanted to treat mum, Helena, to something special. Helena came along to watch and have a taste.

SERVES 4

FOR THE *BRÛLÉE*
100 g (4 oz) almond ratafias
250 g (9 oz) seedless green grapes
2 oranges
2 nectarines, sliced
250 ml (8 fl oz) double cream
2 tablespoons demerara sugar

FOR THE SAUCE
225 (8 oz) strawberries, hulled
Juice of 1/2 orange
1 tablespoon icing sugar
200 ml (7 fl oz) crème fraîche
3 tablespoons Greek yoghurt

TO DECORATE
Icing sugar
Cocoa powder

Pre-heat the grill to a medium heat. For the *brûlée*, crumble the ratafias, reserve 2 tablespoons and spread the remainder over the base of an ovenproof, shallow dish. Sprinkle over half the grapes. With a sharp knife, cut the zest and pith off the oranges and slice the flesh. Layer over the grapes in the dish, with the sliced nectarines. Pour over the cream and sprinkle over the sugar. Place under grill for 10–12 minutes, to caramelize the sugar.

Meanwhile, for the trifles, put the reserved ratafias in the base of two wine glasses.

For the swirl, reserve two large whole strawberries and place the rest in a liquidizer or food processor. Add half the orange juice and the icing sugar and purée to form a smooth coulis.

Spoon the remaining orange juice over the ratafias in the wine glasses, add three-quarters of the remaining grapes and half the crème fraîche. Spoon over half the strawberry coulis.

In a bowl, mix the remaining crème fraîche with the yoghurt. Spoon this over one half of a serving plate, spoon the remaining coulis over the other half and, with a fork, swirl the two together to make a pattern. Halve the two remaining strawberries, make a pile of these and the remaining grapes in the centre and sprinkle with icing sugar.

Remove the hot pudding from the grill and sprinkle with a little cocoa powder. Serve the three desserts.

LESLEY WATERS

A TRIFLE DIFFERENT AND EXOTIC FRUIT HOT-POT

Pineapple and ginger meringue trifle and stewed exotic fruit

Chris Dowling could never be bothered to make sweets but, when he goes out, desserts take precedence over all other courses! He needed a quick and simple pudding that he could make at home.

SERVES 6

FOR THE MERINGUE TRIFLE
4 size-3 egg whites
225 (8 oz) caster sugar
1 Jamaican ginger cake, cut in 1 cm ($1/2$ in) slices
432 g (15 oz) tin of pineapple pieces in natural juice
1 orange, peeled and sliced
Juice of 1 orange

FOR THE HOT-POT
8 tablespoons granulated sugar
300 ml (10 fl oz) water
1 cinnamon stick
1 bay leaf
$1/2$ lemon, juice and zest
$1/2$ orange, juice and zest
1 star fruit, sliced widthways
1 tablespoon white wine
1 pawpaw, peeled, seeded and sliced
225 g (8 oz) strawberries, hulled and halved
Greek yoghurt, to serve (optional)

DESSERTS

Pre-heat the oven to gas mark 6, 200°C, 400°F. Put the egg whites in a clean, grease-free bowl and whisk to stiff peaks. Gradually whisk in the caster sugar and continue whisking until the meringue mixture is very thick and glossy.

Lay the slices of ginger cake in the base of a large ovenproof dish and then pour the pineapple pieces and some of the juice from the tin over the cake. Scatter the orange slices and juice of one orange over the pineapple. Spoon the meringue mixture over the top and cover loosely with foil. Bake in the oven for 5 minutes, until the meringue is golden. Remove the foil and bake for a further 10 minutes.

Put the granulated sugar, water, cinnamon, bay leaf and lemon and orange zest in a large pan and simmer for 5 minutes until syrupy. Add the star fruit, wine and juice of the half-orange and half-lemon. Simmer for 2 minutes. Add the pawpaw and strawberries and simmer for 3 minutes.

Spoon the exotic fruit hot-pot into a serving bowl and serve with Greek yoghurt, if you like. Serve the meringue trifle separately.

LESLEY WATERS

CHARLOTTE'S CHOCOLATE PASSION

Chocolate roulade with kirsch-flavoured cream, black cherries and a chocolate and cherry sauce

Charlotte confessed that she and her husband both had a sweet tooth and said they would love another way of eating chocolate. She also admitted to having been a bit slack on cooking since the arrival of their new baby – the night before she'd fed her husband just on toast!

SERVES 6–8	300 ml (10 fl oz) double cream
3 eggs	Miniature bottle or 4 tablespoons of kirsch
100 g (4 oz) caster sugar	100 g (4 oz) luxury dark chocolate
50 g (2 oz) plain flour	425 g (15 oz) tin of pitted black cherries
25 g (1 oz) cocoa	

TO DECORATE   Mint sprigs
Icing sugar

Pre-heat the oven to gas mark 6, 200°C, 400°F. Break the eggs into a mixing bowl, add the sugar and whisk with an electric whisk, until pale and fluffy. Sift the flour and cocoa together and, with a tablespoon, very gently fold them in, without knocking out the air.

Line a swiss roll tin with baking parchment and pour in the mixture. Gently smooth out to the corners. Bake for about 8–10 minutes, until just firm. Cool in the tin for a few minutes then turn out on a wire rack and leave to cool further.

Whisk the cream until just thick and stir in half the kirsch.

Melt the chocolate in a bowl over a pan of boiling water. Make an icing bag from a triangle of greaseproof paper. Spoon in a tablespoon of melted chocolate, pipe shapes on to a sheet of greaseproof paper and chill.

Stir the remaining kirsch into the melted chocolate, with 2 tablespoons of the cherry juice (add extra if the sauce is too thick). Pour the sauce into a jug and keep warm, to serve with the dessert.

Remove the sponge from the tin on to a work surface. Spread the sponge with the cream. Drain the cherries and spoon on top of the cream. Start rolling it up lengthways, peeling off the paper as you go.

Lift the roulade on to a serving plate and dredge with a little icing sugar. Peel the chocolate shapes off the paper and lay them on top of the roll. Decorate the side of the plate with mint sprigs.

DESSERTS

LESLEY WATERS

PASSION FOR PINEAPPLE

Pineapple and orange *mille feuilles* and stuffed fresh pineapple

Addicted to puddings and chocolate, Ann Frances from Wakefield brought along her favourite
ingredients, with a tub of fromage frais 'to counteract the chocolate'.

SERVES 2	50 g (2 oz) blanched whole almonds
350 g (12 oz) ready-to-roll puff pastry	100 g (4 oz) continental plain chocolate
3 oranges	300 ml (10 fl oz) double cream
4 tablespoons sugar	1 tablespoon icing sugar
1 medium fresh pineapple	200 g (7 oz) light fromage frais or crème
25 g (1 oz) butter	fraîche, to serve

Pre-heat the oven to gas mark 6, 200°C, 400°F. On a lightly floured
surface, roll out the puff pastry to a 30 cm (12 in) by 20 cm (8 in)
oblong, 5 mm (¼ in) thick. Lift on to a greased baking sheet, prick all
over and bake for 8 minutes. When it is golden and risen, remove
from the oven and trim off the edges. Then cut the pastry into three
widthways and put to one side.

Meanwhile, remove the zest from the oranges. In a small pan, put
the orange zest and sugar. Cover with water and leave to simmer
over a gentle heat, until the sugar has dissolved.

To prepare the pineapple, cut it lengthways, keeping the leaves
intact. Hollow out both sides. Cut half the flesh into cubes, roughly
chop the remainder and keep separately to one side.

Heat the butter in a large pan and toast the almonds, until golden.
Add the roughly chopped pineapple and heat through. Add the
orange and sugar mixture. Mix together and keep warm.

Melt the chocolate in a double boiler. Meanwhile, whip the cream
until it holds its shape. Then peel the oranges and slice them.

To assemble, spread one-third of the cream on one piece of the pastry, put half the pineapple cubes and orange slices on the cream and drizzle over 2 tablespoons of the melted chocolate. Put another layer of pastry on top and repeat. Finish with the third layer of pastry and dust with icing sugar.

Spoon the pineapple and nut mixture into one half of the hollowed-out pineapple and drizzle over the remaining chocolate. Serve with the fromage frais or crème fraîche.

KEVIN WOODFORD

LOUISE'S PASSION

Poached meringues with *crème anglaise* and fresh orange

A true pudding-lover, Louise wanted to give Kevin a real challenge, with unusual and exotic fruits, including a couple she'd never even heard of herself until she spotted them in the supermarket!

SERVES 2	1 tablespoon caster sugar
FOR THE MERINGUES	300 ml (10 fl oz) milk
300 ml (10 fl oz) milk	1 grenadillo
Vanilla pod, halved	1 orange
2 eggs whites	1 mango, stoned and chopped finely
100 g (4 oz) caster sugar	10 physalis (Cape gooseberries), husks peeled back
FOR THE *CRÈME ANGLAISE*	2 tablespoons flaked almonds, to decorate
2 egg yolks	

Pour half the milk into a saucepan, heat gently with half the vanilla pod.

Pre-heat the grill to a hot heat. Spread the almonds on a baking tray and brown under the grill for 2 minutes, until golden. Set aside.

Whisk the egg whites until stiff and gradually add the caster sugar, until you have a soft meringue. Warm two tablespoons in hot water and scoop out a spoonful of the egg-white mixture. Mould into an egg-shaped quenelle, using the spoons and drop gently into the heated milk. Bring the milk to the boil and cook for 2–3 minutes. Then remove to a plate. Repeat to make a further quenelle.

Meanwhile, make the *crème anglaise* (custard) in a bain-marie. Put the 2 egg yolks, and a tablespoon of caster sugar in a bowl and set the bowl over a saucepan of boiling water. Heat the remaining milk with the other half of the vanilla pod in a pan to just below boiling point. Remove the vanilla pod. Then add the milk to the egg mixture and whisk constantly over the pan of water until slightly thickened. It should thinly coat the back of a wooden spoon.

Cut the grenadillo in half and scoop the soft, seedy centre into the *crème anglaise*. Reserve one half for decoration.

Use the zest of the orange as a garnish and peel the segments.

To serve, spoon the *crème anglaise* on to a plate. Arrange the orange segments and mango around the plate and place the meringues on top. Garnish with the physalis and browned almonds.

K E V I N   W O O D F O R D

GABRIELLA'S PEARS ON A BED OF HOT CHOCOLATE SCONES WITH ZABAGLIONE

Chocolate scones with apple purée, poached pears and zabaglione

Gabriella asked Kevin to create something that would tempt boyfriend John to propose – after ten years of courting!

SERVES 2
FOR THE SCONES
50 g (2 oz) butter
100 g (4 oz) plain flour, sifted
1 tablespoon caster sugar
1 tablespoon chocolate chips

50 ml (2 fl oz) milk

FOR THE PEARS
2 pears, peeled
450 ml (15 fl oz) white wine
4 tablespoons caster sugar

FOR THE APPLE PURÉE
5 apples, peeled and quartered
300 ml (10 fl oz) water
1 teaspoon ground cinnamon
1 tablespoon caster sugar

FOR THE ZABAGLIONE
3 yolks
2 tablespoons caster sugar
75 g (3 oz) butter, melted
Lemon juice
Apple slices, sprig of mint, to garnish (optional)

Pre-heat the oven to gas mark 6, 200°C, 400°F. Rub the butter and flour together, until the mixture resembles breadcrumbs. Add the sugar and chocolate chips and enough milk to gather the mixture together, to form a dough. Divide into two equal balls and make each into a 10 cm (4 in) round scone. Place on a greased baking sheet and bake for 10–12 minutes.

Put the pears in a saucepan, with the wine and caster sugar. Bring to the boil and then simmer gently, with the lid on, for 15 minutes. Remove the pears from the wine and hollow out the bottom of each pear, so it will stand up.

Cook the apples in the water, with a pinch of cinnamon and the caster sugar. Bring to the boil and then leave to simmer for 10–12 minutes, until the apples are soft. Beat to a smooth purée over a high heat.

To make the zabaglione, whisk the egg yolks in a bowl over a pan of boiling water for 1 minute. Add the caster sugar and continue to whisk over the heat, until the mixture starts to thicken and turn white in colour. Slowly add the melted butter, whisking constantly. Stir in a squeeze of lemon juice and set aside the zabaglione.

Pre-heat the grill to hot. Place the scones on a plate. Spoon the apple purée on top and then put a pear on the apple. Pour the zabaglione over and grill for 2 minutes. Serve while still warm, garnished with apple slices and a sprig of mint, if you like.

K E V I N   W O O D F O R D

RACHEL'S RUDE AND RASPBERRY PUDDING

Dried fruit steamed pudding with raspberry cream sauce

With her first wedding anniversary just around the corner, Rachel Williams wanted something 'naughty but nice' to make sure that she and husband Bruce made it to their second anniversary.

SERVES 4
FOR THE PUDDING
50 g (2 oz) mixed dried fruit, e.g. prunes, figs and apricots, chopped
50 g (2 oz) butter, softened
100 g (4 oz) soft light brown sugar
2 eggs, beaten
100 g (4 oz) self-raising flour, sifted

2 tablespoons milk
2 tablespoons golden syrup

FOR THE RASPBERRY CREAM
290 g (10^1/$_2$ oz) tin of raspberries in apple juice, drained and juice reserved
300 ml (10 fl oz) double cream
Dried fruit, sliced, to garnish (optional)

Soak the dried fruit in the juice from the tin of raspberries.

Mix together the butter and sugar in a bowl, with a wooden spoon, until they have creamed and turned a pale yellow. Beat in the eggs, little by little. If the mixture begins to curdle add a tablespoon of the flour. Once the eggs are fully incorporated, fold in the flour gradually. Add the milk. Stir in the soaked fruit (reserve the juice).

Put the golden syrup into the bottom of a buttered 2-pint, heatproof pudding basin. Spoon the sponge mixture on top, cover with microwave-safe cling film, pierce and microwave for 4 minutes at full power. Leave to stand for 5 minutes.

To make the raspberry sauce, mash the raspberries with a fork. Stir in the double cream. Whisk to thicken the cream.

To serve, invert the sponge on to a plate. Serve with the raspberry sauce. Surround the pudding with slices of dried fruit, if you like.

KEVIN WOODFORD

COPACABANA PUDDING

Kumquat, pineapple and apple crumble with custard

Part-time jazz-singer, Gina Browne, wanted a pudding to tempt her husband Jonathan, whom she met when she went into his shop to buy a pair of trousers.

SERVES 4
FOR THE CRUMBLE
50 g (2 oz) shelled mixed nuts
75 g (3 oz) plain flour
50 g (2 oz) demerara sugar
50 g (2 oz) butter

FOR THE FILLING
25 g (1 oz) butter
100 g (4 oz) kumquats, quartered
1 star fruit, chopped
50 g (2 oz) soft light brown sugar
2 dessert apples, peeled, cored and chopped

150 g (5 oz) fresh pineapple, cut in chunks, or a 200 g (7 oz) tin of pineapple chunks, drained

FOR THE CUSTARD SAUCE
450 ml (15 fl oz) milk
4 eggs
25 g (1 oz) caster sugar
1 passion-fruit, halved

TO DECORATE
Slices of lime
Mint sprigs

Pre-heat the oven to gas mark 7, 220°C, 425°F. Dry-fry the nuts in a frying-pan for 3 minutes, stirring frequently, until golden. Put in a food processor and process until roughly chopped. Add the flour and sugar and mix well. Add the butter and process until the mixture looks like coarse breadcrumbs.

For the filling, melt the butter in a large frying-pan. Add the kumquats and cook for 2 minutes, stirring occasionally. Add the star fruit and sugar and cook for 2 minutes more. Continue to stir occasionally. Add the apples and cook for 2 minutes. Stir in the pineapple chunks and cook for 5 minutes.

Spoon the fruit mixture into four 10 cm (4 in) glass ovenproof ramekin dishes. Top with the crumble and stand on a baking tray.

Bake for 8–10 minutes, until the crumble topping is golden.

Meanwhile, make the custard sauce, by gently heating the milk to just below boiling point in a pan. Put the eggs in a heatproof bowl, place over a pan of boiling water (the water must not touch the bowl) and whisk for 3 minutes. Add the caster sugar and whisk by hand for a further 3 minutes. Slowly pour the hot milk over the eggs and sugar, whisking all the time.

Scoop the pulp and seeds out of the passion-fruit and stir them into the custard. Continue whisking for 5 minutes, until the custard is thick enough to coat the back of a spoon. Taste and add a little more sugar if necessary. Serve the tropical-fruit crumbles with the passion-fruit custard and decorate with slices of lime and sprigs of mint.

K E V I N   W O O D F O R D

BANANADRAMA

Banana and custard baked meringue, banana gratin and banana custard

Despite breaking one of her eggs while tipping out her ingredients, Pat from Preston was stunned when Kevin, one egg down, still managed to create not one, not two but three amazing puddings in just 20 minutes!

SERVES 4–6
FOR THE MERINGUE
1 oblong Madeira cake
Grated zest from 1 lemon and 1 lime
1 banana, sliced
3 tablespoons strawberry jam
200 g (7 oz) caster sugar
150 ml (5 fl oz) white wine
Juice and zest of 1 orange
3 eggs, separated
300 ml (10 fl oz) milk

$^1/_2$ teaspoon vanilla essence

FOR THE GRATIN
2 bananas
25 g (1 oz) butter
1 tablespoon demerara sugar
$^1/_2$ teaspoon grated nutmeg

FOR THE BANANA CUSTARD
1 banana, sliced
Slices of orange, to decorate

Pre-heat the oven to gas mark 7, 220°C, 425°F. Slice off a quarter of the cake, put into a food processor and blend to form crumbs; set aside. Slice the remaining cake into fingers and put in an ovenproof pudding dish. Sprinkle over the lemon and lime zest and one banana, sliced. Dot over the jam.

Meanwhile, dissolve 100 g (4 oz) of the sugar in the wine in a saucepan over a low heat, add half of the orange juice and all the zest and pour over the cake in the dish.

To make the custard, put the egg yolks in a bowl and set the bowl over a pan of boiling water. With an electric whisk, whisk until pale. Add 50 g (2 oz) of the sugar in three stages, whisking continuously, until pale, fluffy and thickened. Remove from the heat. Meanwhile, heat the milk to just below boiling and pour into the mixture slowly, whisking continuously. Add the vanilla essence. Pour about half the custard on to the dish.

Whisk the egg whites to stiff peaks and then whisk in the remaining sugar. Pipe or spoon the meringue on to the custard and bake for 6–8 minutes, until browned.

For the gratin, slice the bananas in half lengthways and then slice thinly. Melt the butter in a frying-pan and add the demerara sugar, the remaining orange juice, the nutmeg and the banana. Cook together for 2 minutes and then transfer to a small ovenproof dish. Spoon over most of the remaining custard, reserving about 3 tablespoons. Sprinkle over the reserved cake crumbs and put into the oven for 5 minutes to warm through and brown the topping.

Put the sliced banana into an individual serving dish and add the reserved custard. Garnish with an orange twist. Serve with the other two desserts.

INDEX

D

duck
  crisp-griddled with savoury rice,
      sweet and sour sauce, stir-fried
      vegetables and 'seaweed'
      55-6
  golden duck legs with parsnip
      sauce, saffron rice and sesame
      broccoli 61-2
dumplings, herby 56-7

F

fennel and potato rösti 25-6
feta toasties with salsa 14-15
filo pastry
  cod in a creamy sauce, baked in
      filo pastry and served with
      mushroom sauce 40-1
  filo roulade 14-15
  tomato and cheese parcels 27-8
fish
  creamy curry with savoury rice and
      spicy green beans 32-3
  medley of fresh fish on a bed of
      chablis and spring onion
      sauce 42-3
fruit, dried steamed pudding with
    raspberry cream sauce 89

G

ginger and pineapple meringue trifle
    and stewed exotic fruit 82-3
gnocchi with tomato sauce,
    semolina 20-1
green beans
  cardamom beans 30-1
  spicy 32-3

H

haddock mousses with white wine
    and cream sauce and baby
    vegetables 38-9
hog's pudding, sliced white with
    warm potato salad and sweet and
    sour red cabbage 64-5
hoummos 48-9

K

kumquats
  kumquat marmalade 53-4
  kumquat, pineapple and apple
      crumble with custard 90-1

L

lamb
  minced lamb kebabs with
      vegetables in wine, spinach
      and orange salad and
      creamed spinach 65-6
  mouthwatering Mediterranean
      magic 68-9
lasagne, spinach and mushroom
    12-13
leeks, orange 56-7
lobster in wine and cream sauce,
    with herby savoury rice 36-7

M

meringues
  cinnamon, poached peaches, and
      iced raspberry cream 79-80
  poached with crème anglaise and
      fresh orange 86-7
mushrooms
  cod baked in filo pastry with

READY STEADY COOK 4

READY STEADY COOK 4

AINSLEY HARRIOTT

ROSS BURDEN

PHOTOGRAPHS BY
JULIET PIDDINGTON

BBC BOOKS

This book is published to accompany the television series *Ready Steady Cook*
which is produced by Bazal Productions Ltd for the BBC

Executive Producer: Linda Clifford
Producer: Mary Ramsay

Published by BBC Books, an imprint of BBC Worldwide Ltd,
Woodlands, 80 Wood Lane, London, W12 0TT

First published in 1997
Compiled by Bazal Productions Ltd
Recipes copyright © Ainsley Harriott and Ross Burden 1997
Photographs by Juliet Piddington, copyright © BBC Worldwide Publishing 1997
Home Economist: Sarah Ramsbottom

ISBN 0 563 38362 3

Designed by Louise Morley
Printed by Martins the Printers Ltd, Berwick-upon-Tweed
Bound by Hunter & Foulis Ltd, Edinburgh
Colour separation by Radstock Reproductions Ltd, Midsomer Norton
Colour printing by Lawrence Allen Ltd, Weston-super-Mare
Cover printed by Belmont Press Ltd, Northampton

CONTENTS

INTRODUCTION

Well, we've made over 300 programmes, survived two fires in one show and I've had half a pint of cream squirted in my face. It's been another fun-packed year on **Ready Steady Cook**. Doesn't time fly?

And as regular viewers of **Ready Steady Cook** must know by now, I am not the world's greatest cook, but I am always on hand to advise chefs on how to make instant mashed potato and the best thing to do with a gravy granule. Now they are things I know how to cook.

But I still do occasionally try and have a go at all the lovely recipes that our chefs rustle up on the programme and always keep my **Ready Steady Cook** recipe books on hand. And here's yet another delicious selection, this time from Ainsley and Ross, to give me a bit of incentive to get in the kitchen. I hope it works for you.

Happy cooking!

Presenter, **Ready Steady Cook**

A Note on Ingredients and Techniques

Good-quality ingredients make all the difference to the taste of the finished dish. For best results, choose unsalted butter and extra virgin olive oil. Buy ripe, flavoursome tomatoes, and whenever possible, really fresh herbs. If a recipe specifies dried herbs, freeze-dried ones usually have the best flavour. For desserts, chocolate should contain at least 50 per cent cocoa solids — check the back of the wrapper.

> Some of the recipes contain raw or lightly cooked eggs. Because of the slight risk of salmonella poisoning, these should be avoided by the sick, the elderly, the very young, and pregnant women. The chances of contamination are greatly reduced if you buy free-range eggs, preferably organic, from a reputable supplier.

Many of the recipes in this book include wine. Use a wine that you would enjoy drinking rather than cheap 'cooking' wine — if it's not worth drinking it's not worth cooking with! You can use unsweetened apple juice or stock if you prefer.

The chefs on **Ready Steady Cook** often cook on a ridged grill pan. Ridged grill pans are made of cast iron and usually have a spout for pouring off the cooking juices. They are a very healthy way of cooking because the ridges keep the food raised above any fat that runs off. They also make attractive grill marks on food — to make a criss-cross pattern, give the food a half-turn halfway through cooking each side. Use ridged grill pans for steaks, chops, fish or chunky slices of vegetables such as aubergines, courgettes or peppers.

Finally, **Ready Steady Cook** is all about putting together a delicious meal from whatever ingredients you have to hand. The recipes in this book are proof that some of the most memorable dishes are the ones that come about on the spur of the moment. So, if you don't have a particular ingredient, follow the example of our chefs and improvise. Don't be afraid to get in the kitchen and **Ready Steady Cook!**

If you are trying to cut calories or reduce the fat in your diet it doesn't mean you have to miss out on taste or cooking these recipes. Check out some healthy alternatives. Buy trimmed or extra lean meat and bacon and remove the skin from chicken pieces. Use half-fat hard cheeses and semi-skimmed milk.
For everyday use, why not try low-fat fromage frais and low-fat natural yoghurt as substitutes for cream and crème fraiche.
Opt for low-fat soft cheese or quark instead of cream cheese.
Cook with sunflower, vegetable or olive oil in place of butter where possible.

LARDER INGREDIENTS USED ON
READY STEADY COOK

Arrowroot	Fresh chives	Olive oil
Baking powder	Fresh coriander	Oranges
Balsamic vinegar	Fresh dill	Paprika
Bay leaves	Fresh mint	Peppercorns
Beef stock cubes	Fresh parsley	Plain flour
Bottle of red wine	Fresh rosemary	Red-wine vinegar
Bottle of white wine	Fresh sage	Salt
Cardamom pods	Fresh thyme	Self-raising flour
Caster sugar	Fresh white bread	Sesame oil
Cayenne pepper	Garam masala	Soft brown sugar
Chicken stock cubes	Garlic	Soy sauce
Chilli powder	Golden syrup	Sunflower oil
Clear honey	Granulated sugar	Tabasco sauce
Cocoa powder	Greek yoghurt	Tomato purée
Cornflour	Ground all-spice	Tomato sauce
Demerara sugar	Ground cinnamon	Turmeric
Dijon mustard	Ground coriander	Unsalted butter
Double cream	Ground cumin	Vegetable stock cubes
Dried mixed herbs	Ground ginger	Vanilla essence
Dried oregano	Ground nutmeg	Vanilla pod
Eggs, size 3	Icing Sugar	White-wine vinegar
Fresh basil	Lemons/limes	Wholegrain mustard
Fresh chervil	Milk	Worcestershire sauce

VEGETARIAN DISHES

THE STAR OF CHRISTMAS – 10

SANDAL BURGERS – 12

NIGHTMARE ON PUMPKIN STREET – 14

GOOD ENOUGH TO GET OUT OF BED FOR – 15

NUREYEV'S HALLOWE'EN PUMPKIN AND GLAZED
TOFFEE APPLES – 17

ESCORT TERRACE RISOTTO WITH THREE
CHIMNEYS – 18

EDWARD'S MARVELLOUS MUSHROOMS – 19

FRANTIC BROCCOLI AND CHEESE SOUFFLÉS – 21

ROSS BURDEN

THE STAR OF CHRISTMAS

Star-shaped chestnut pastries, with stuffed mushrooms and
creamy celery sauce
See photograph

**Weight-Watchers lecturer, Maralyn Braybrook, asked Ross for a healthy meal
for Christmas as she had to be seen to be good in case any of her 'pupils' were watching!**

SERVES 4	350 ml (12 fl oz) white wine
450 g (1 lb) puff pastry	5 celery sticks, cut in 2.5 cm (1 inch) lengths
435 g (15¼ oz) can of chestnut purée	3 tablespoons double cream
1 egg, beaten	2 tablespoons snipped fresh chives
225 g (8 oz) button mushrooms	25 g (1 oz) butter
4 tablespoons olive oil	Salt and freshly ground black pepper
1 onion, finely chopped	Sprigs of flatleaf parsley, chives and celery
100 g (4 oz) Stilton cheese, crumbled	leaves, to garnish
50 g (2 oz) walnut halves, roughly chopped	

Pre-heat the oven to gas mark 7,220°C,425°F. Roll out half of the
pastry on a lightly floured surface to a 25 cm (10 inch) square about 5
mm (¼ inch) thick and cut into four squares. Repeat with the other half of
the pastry. Spoon 4 tablespoons of chestnut purée in the centre of one
piece of pastry. Brush the edges of the pastry with beaten egg and
cover with another piece of pastry. Press the edges together to seal well.

Place a bowl measuring about 11.5 cm (4½ inches) over the top
and use as a guide to cut the pastry into a circle. Cut a zig-zag
around the edge, to give a star shape. Score the top of the star from
the centre to the zig-zag border, at 1 cm (½ inch) intervals. Brush with
more beaten egg and put on a greased baking sheet. Repeat, to
make four stars. Bake for 12–15 minutes, until the pastry is well risen
and golden.

Remove the stalks from the mushrooms and make a hollow in each cap. Chop the stalks roughly. Heat 2 tablespoons of oil in a pan, add the onion and cook for 3 minutes, stirring occasionally. Add the mushroom stalks and cook for 2 minutes. Stir in the Stilton and walnuts and season with pepper. Spoon the mixture into the mushroom caps. Heat the other 2 tablespoons of oil in a frying-pan, add the filled mushrooms and cook for 3 minutes. Pour 150 ml (5 fl oz) of wine into the pan, cover and cook gently for 8 minutes.

Put the celery, remaining wine and some salt and pepper in a pan and simmer for 8–10 minutes, until softened. Put in a food processor, with the cream, and process until smooth. Push through a sieve back into the pan, add the chives and butter and heat until the butter has melted.

To serve, put the chestnut stars on a serving plate and place the filled mushrooms, with their cooking juices, to one side. Spoon the celery sauce around the edge of the chestnut stars and garnish with sprigs of flatleaf parsley, chives and celery leaves.

READY STEADY COOK Tips

Steamed spinach and ricotta cheese could be used in place of chestnut purée.

Parsley is the most widely used herb and there are now two kinds available. Flatleaf parsley is regarded as less bitter and has a fuller flavour than the more common curly parsley. Flatleaf is great in salads, but can be interchanged with curly in almost any savoury dish. Don't throw away the stalks; their concentrated flavour is ideal for use in a bouqet garni to flavour stock, soups and casseroles.

ROSS BURDEN

SANDAL BURGERS

Sheila Lawson had been vegetarian for 8 years but had always avoided tofu as she had absolutely no idea what to do with it. 'It never looks very appetizing!' she said. Ross managed, of course, to change her mind.

SERVES 2

FOR THE SAUCE

1 red pepper, quartered and seeded
6 tablespoons olive oil
1 tablespoon white-wine vinegar

FOR THE BURGERS

50 g (2 oz) cashew nuts
225 g (8 oz) smoked tofu
1 garlic clove, crushed
2 eggs
Handful of fresh coriander leaves
1 teaspoon soy sauce

1 tablespoon sunflower oil
Sprigs of chervil or parsley, to garnish

FOR THE STIR-FRY

100 g (4 oz) long-grain rice
200 g (7 oz) mixed baby corn and mangetout
2 tablespoons sesame oil
3 spring onions, chopped
3 tablespoons snipped fresh chives
3 tablespoons soy sauce
Salt and freshly ground black pepper
Fresh chervil and coriander, to garnish

Pre-heat the oven to gas mark 7, 220°C, 425°F. Cook the rice for the stir-fry in salted, boiling water for 10–12 minutes, until tender. Drain and reserve. Put the pepper on a baking tray and roast for about 10 minutes. Put in a plastic bag until cool enough to handle.

Toast the cashew nuts in a dry frying-pan over a high heat, until golden brown, shaking continuously. In a food processor, process the tofu, garlic and cashew nuts roughly and then add the eggs, coriander leaves and soy sauce. Process again, to form a thick mixture. Flour your hands well and shape the mixture into four burgers. Heat the sunflower oil in a frying-pan and cook the burgers for 2 minutes on each side.

Remove the skin from the roast red pepper. Put the flesh into the clean processor bowl, together with the olive oil and vinegar, and process until smooth.

Slice the baby corn and mangetout diagonally into chunks and cook in salted, boiling water for 3 minutes. Drain. Heat the sesame oil in a wok and add the spring onions, baby corn and mangetout; cook for 1–2 minutes and then add the rice, chives and soy sauce. Season. Stir-fry for 3–4 minutes, until heated through.

To serve, drizzle the pepper sauce round the outside of the plate, pile the tofu burgers in the centre and garnish with sprigs of chervil or parsley. Serve the rice in a bowl, garnished with coriander and chervil leaves.

READY STEADY COOK Tips

You could grill the peppers under a hot grill for 10–12 minutes, instead of roasting them, to avoid heating the oven. Alternatively, hold the pepper over a gas flame on a skewer, until the skin is blackened.

Put the roasted/grilled pepper in a plastic bag or in a bowl covered with cling film and leave for a few minutes. The skin will come away easily.

ROSS BURDEN

NIGHTMARE ON PUMPKIN STREET

Pumpkin ravioli with sage butter sauce

Our Hallowe'en contestant, Amanda Ward-Baker, told Fern she was bullied to come on the show by her daughters Ebony-Rose and Ella — our number one fans. Spookily, even their goldfish are called Ainsley and Lesley!

SERVES 2

FOR THE PASTA
225 g (8 oz) plain flour
2 eggs
Salt

FOR THE FILLING
1 tablespoon mixed candied peel
50 g (2 oz) flaked almonds
250 g (9 oz) ricotta
¼ pumpkin, peeled, seeded and chopped

1 egg yolk
1 egg, lightly beaten
Salt

FOR THE SAUCE
100 g (4 oz) butter
2 tablespoons chopped fresh sage
Grated nutmeg
1 tablespoon freshly grated Parmesan, to serve
Fresh sage leaves, to garnish

To make the pasta, put the flour, eggs and a pinch of salt in a food processor and process until the mixture resembles breadcrumbs. Put the mixture on to the work surface and work it together. Lightly knead, cover with cling film and leave to one side to rest.

Meanwhile, in a food processor, process the mixed peel and almonds for 10 seconds. Add the ricotta, pumpkin flesh and egg yolk and process until smooth.

Divide the pasta dough into four. Roll out each piece thinly to a rectangle about 25 cm x 20 cm (10 inches x 8 inches), using either a pasta machine or a rolling pin. Lay the pasta on the floured work surface and put 2 teaspoons of the pumpkin mixture in an even row on two of the sheets. Brush round the filling with the beaten egg. Place the other two sheets on top and press round each mound of filling, to seal well. Using a 5 cm (2 inch) pastry cutter, cut round each mound. Bring a pan of salted water to the boil and cook the pasta for 3 minutes.

Meanwhile, melt the butter in a small pan and, when bubbling, add the sage and season with nutmeg. Drain the pasta and put on to a serving plate. Pour over the butter sauce. Sprinkle over the Parmesan and garnish with sage leaves.

READY STEADY COOK Tips

Make sure the ravioli are well sealed before cooking or they will come apart in the water.

Parmigiano Reggiano is the very best Parmesan you can buy. Grate it or, if you prefer, shave it with a vegetable peeler and scatter over pasta, salads and vegetables. Grano Padano is almost as good but not quite as tasty. Store your chunk of Parmesan in the fridge or freezer, wrapped in foil.

ROSS BURDEN

GOOD ENOUGH TO GET OUT OF BED FOR

Deep-fried aubergine slices with feta filling, filo money bags and two pepper relishes

Julia Walker confessed to Ross that she is incredibly lazy in the kitchen. She can never be bothered to cook, and has had a washing machine for over a year and still doesn't know how to use it. Ross thought this was just the thing to ease her in gently.

SERVES 2
½ aubergine, thinly sliced
1 red pepper, seeded and quartered

1 yellow pepper, seeded and quartered
3 tablespoons olive oil
75 g (3 oz) butter

½ onion, thinly sliced
1 tablespoon balsamic vinegar
2 teaspoons brown sugar
1 sheet fresh filo pastry
6 fresh chives
1 courgette
Juice of 1 lemon

Oil, for deep-frying
200 g (7 oz) feta
3 tablespoons Greek yoghurt
1 tablespoon chopped fresh basil
2 tomatoes, skinned, seeded and diced
Salt and freshly ground black pepper

Pre-heat the oven to gas mark 7, 220°C, 425°F. Put the aubergine slices in a colander, sprinkle with salt and leave to drain, to extract the bitter juices.

Put the pepper quarters on a baking sheet and roast until the skins blacken. Then put them in a bowl, cover with cling film and leave for 3–5 minutes. Take the skins off and blend the yellow pepper with a tablespoon of olive oil in a processor, until smooth. Transfer to a bowl. Do the same with the red pepper. Keep to one side.

Heat 25 g (1 oz) of butter in a small pan and gently fry the onion until softened. Stir in the vinegar and sugar and caramelize. Keep to one side. Melt the rest of the butter. Cut the sheet of filo into six squares. Grease a baking sheet with some of the melted butter and put the filo squares on the sheet. Place a teaspoon of onion mixture in the centre of each square and draw each corner together to create a 'money bag'. Tie each with a chive. Brush the money bags with more melted butter and cook in the oven for 4 minutes, or until the pastry is golden.

Cut the courgette into long, thin strips and put them in a large mixing bowl. Pour on the last tablespoon of olive oil and the lemon juice. Season. Put a smaller bowl inside, to press down the courgette.

Meanwhile, heat a deep pan with the oil. Rinse the aubergine slices and drain them well on kitchen paper. Deep-fry for 2–3 minutes, until golden and crisp.

Put the feta, Greek yoghurt and basil in a blender and process until smooth.

In the centre of the plate, layer the aubergine and the feta mixture. Arrange the filo parcels around the plate. Spoon on the pepper relishes and scatter on the courgette and tomato pieces.

A I N S L E Y   H A R R I O T T

NUREYEV'S HALLOWE'EN PUMPKIN AND GLAZED TOFFEE APPLES

Vegetable curry served in a pumpkin, with caramelized apple rings and yoghurt

Georgina Ward does all the cooking at home because 'it gives me time by myself – I can get away from baby and husband and shut myself in the kitchen with a glass of red wine, Prokofiev and oodles of garlic.'

SERVES 4

FOR THE PUMPKIN

1.5 kg (3 lb) pumpkin
350 g (12 oz) potatoes, cut in 2 cm (¾ inch) cubes
2 tablespoons olive oil
1 onion, chopped
1 garlic clove, finely chopped
8 cardamom pods
2 teaspoons curry powder
Pinch of ground cloves
225 g (8 oz) tomatoes, cut into wedges
1 tablespoon chopped fresh coriander
Salt and freshly ground black pepper
Sprigs of fresh coriander, to garnish

FOR THE TOFFEE APPLES

4 dessert apples, cored and cut in 1 cm (½ inch) rings
Juice of 1 lemon
4 tablespoons icing sugar
½ teaspoon ground cinnamon
225 g (8 oz) Greek yoghurt

Pre-heat the oven to gas mark 6, 200°C, 400°F. Make zig-zag cuts around the top of the pumpkin and lift off the 'lid'. Scoop out and discard the seeds and then carefully cut out the pumpkin flesh, to leave a 1 cm (½ in) thick shell. Put the pumpkin shell in the oven for 10–15 minutes, until the skin is slightly charred.

Cut the pumpkin flesh into 2 cm (¾ inch) cubes. Cook the pumpkin and potato in boiling water for 6–8 minutes, until almost tender.

Heat the oil in a frying-pan, add the onion, garlic, cardamom pods, curry powder and ground cloves, season with salt and pepper and cook for 4 minutes, stirring occasionally. Drain the pumpkin and potatoes and add to the frying-pan, with the tomatoes and coriander. Season with salt and pepper. Cook for a further 5 minutes, stirring occasionally. Spoon the vegetable curry into the pumpkin shell and garnish with sprigs of coriander.

Put the apple rings on a baking tray and sprinkle over the lemon juice and icing sugar. Put under a hot grill for 5–8 minutes, until the apple rings have caramelized. Sprinkle the cinnamon over the yoghurt and serve with the glazed toffee apples.

A I N S L E Y   H A R R I O T T

ESCORT TERRACE RISOTTO WITH THREE CHIMNEYS

Student Liz lives with 5 other girls and they each take turns in cooking. Liz's day is Wednesday and she wanted something to impress them with so Ainsley came up with this gorgeous mushroom and cheese risotto.

SERVES 4	1 tablespoon chopped fresh coriander
2 tablespoons olive oil	450 ml (1 pint) vegetable stock
1 onion, chopped	300 g (11 oz) can of garden peas, drained
225 g (8 oz) mushrooms, sliced	6 pick and mix cheeses (2 Boursin, 2 Danish
(keep 3 large ones whole)	blue and 2 Bel Paese), cubed
225 g (8 oz) long-grain white rice	Salt and freshly ground black pepper
150 ml (5 fl oz) white wine	1 lemon and 1 lime, sliced, to garnish (optional)
1 teaspoon ground cumin	Leaves of fresh coriander, to garnish

In a large pan, heat the oil and cook the onion for 3 minutes, until softened. Stir in the sliced mushrooms and cook for a further 2 minutes.

Add the rice, wine, cumin and chopped coriander. Slowly add the stock, stirring occasionally, and cook for 10 minutes, until the rice swells and is tender. Add the peas, cover and cook for a further 5 minutes. Stir in half of the chopped Boursin and Danish blue for the last minute of the cooking time. Pre-heat the grill to hot.

Slice off the stalks of the three whole mushrooms and stuff with the Bel Paese cheese. Place on the grill pan. Shake a little olive oil on to each mushroom, season and grill for 8–10 minutes, until the cheese is melted and the mushrooms have browned.

To serve, put the risotto on a large plate, sprinkle the rest of the cheese over the rice and place the stuffed mushrooms on top.

Garnish with a few leaves of coriander, and slices of lemon and lime, if you like.

A I N S L E Y   H A R R I O T T

EDWARD'S MARVELLOUS MUSHROOMS

Mushrooms stuffed with leek, cheese and nut soufflé, with leek and mushroom lasagne

Student Edward Warren told Ainsley that *Ready Steady Cook* was a cult show in his house. He wanted to cook something a bit posh for his fellow housemates for under a fiver.

SERVES 2	200 ml (7 fl oz) crème fraiche
4 large mushrooms	2 eggs, separated
2 tablespoons olive oil	1½ tablespoons vegetarian Cheddar, grated
100 g (4 oz) walnut pieces	2 tablespoons olive oil
1 leek, sliced	4 small mushrooms, chopped
150 ml (5 fl oz) white wine	4 fresh lasagne sheets
25 g (1 oz) butter	Salt and freshly ground black pepper
50 g (2 oz) plain flour	

Pre-heat the oven to gas mark 7, 220°C, 425°F. Wipe the large mushrooms and remove and discard the stalks. Put the mushrooms on to a baking sheet and drizzle over 1 tablespoon of olive oil. Season and bake for 5 minutes.

Meanwhile, dry-fry the walnuts, until browned, turning occasionally. Heat the remaining tablespoon of olive oil in a pan and sauté the leek for 4 minutes, until softened. Then add 30 ml (1 fl oz) of white wine.

To make the soufflé, melt the butter in a pan. Stir in the flour. Stir in half the crème fraiche and, when thickened, beat in the egg yolks. Whisk the egg whites until stiff. Put half the egg yolk mixture in a bowl. Stir in half the leek, the cheese and 2 tablespoons of the nuts and season. Fold in the egg whites. Put a few nuts on each mushroom. Spoon on the soufflé and bake for 5–6 minutes until golden and risen. Add the remaining crème fraiche and 90 ml (3 fl oz) of white wine to the remaining egg yolk mixture and warm through in a small pan.

Heat a tablespoon of oil in a pan and sauté the chopped mushrooms. Add the remaining leek, remaining 30 ml (1 fl oz) of white wine and any remaining nuts.

Bring a pan of salted water to the boil and cook the lasagne sheets for 1 minute. Drain. Cut each sheet in half.

Put two lasagne strips on each plate. Spoon on the sautéd leeks and the mushrooms and then add a layer of pasta. Spoon on the sauce and drizzle over the remaining tablespoon of olive oil. Serve the soufflés separately.

READY STEADY COOK Tip
If you are feeling really extravagant, use fresh wild mushrooms in place of chopped mushrooms. Packs are available in most large supermarkets and it beats putting on your wellies and going armed with a reference book to gather them yourself.

A I N S L E Y   H A R R I O T T

FRANTIC BROCCOLI AND CHEESE SOUFFLÉS

Broccoli and cheese soufflés, with mushroom croutes
and hollandaise sauce.
See photograph

Annette Pyke told us that she loves cooking but it's wasted at home because husband Steven 'eats like a child – even at Christmas he had sausage and chips instead of turkey.' She added, 'It's like feeding a third child, although the kids' tastes have got sophisticated.'

SERVES 3
FOR THE SOUFFLÉS
2 tablespoons olive oil
4 tablespoons grated Parmesan
275 ml (9 fl oz) milk
25 g (1 oz) butter
25 g (1 oz) plain flour
¼ teaspoon grated nutmeg
225 g (8 oz) broccoli, green florets only, cut into small pieces
150 g (5 oz) Gruyère cheese, grated
3 eggs, separated
Salt and freshly ground black pepper

FOR THE CROUTES
25 g (1 oz) butter
225 g (8 oz) button mushrooms, sliced
75 ml (3 fl oz) double cream
1 tablespoon finely chopped fresh parsley
3–4 tablespoons olive oil
6 slices of French bread, cut on the diagonal

FOR THE SAUCE
2 tablespoons white-wine vinegar
10 peppercorns
3 egg yolks
175 g (6 oz) unsalted butter, melted
Salt and freshly ground black pepper

Pre-heat the oven to gas mark 4, 180°C, 350°F. Brush the insides of six 150 ml (5 fl oz) ramekins with a little oil and coat with 3 tablespoons of the Parmesan cheese. Heat the milk in a pan, until almost simmering.
Heat the butter in a pan and, when bubbling, add the flour and cook for a minute, stirring constantly. Pour in the hot milk and whisk

over a medium heat, until the mixture is smooth and simmering. Remove from the heat and season with grated nutmeg, salt and pepper.

Cook the broccoli for 5–6 minutes until tender, drain and mash just enough to give small pieces. Stir the broccoli, Gruyère and egg yolks into the sauce.

Whisk the egg whites until they form soft peaks and gently fold into the broccoli mixture. Divide between the six ramekins, sprinkle over the remaining tablespoon of grated Parmesan and bake in the oven for 15 minutes, until risen and golden.

For the croutes, heat 25 g (1 oz) of the butter in a pan and sauté the mushrooms for 5 minutes. Season well and stir in the double cream and parsley. Keep warm until ready to serve. In a separate frying-pan, heat 3–4 tablespoons of olive oil and sauté the bread slices, until golden on each side.

To make the hollandaise sauce, heat the white-wine vinegar in a small pan, with 3 tablespoons of water and the peppercorns. Reduce this mixture to a tablespoon and pour into a food processor bowl. Add to this 3 egg yolks. Pour the melted butter slowly into the egg yolk and vinegar mixture, while the processor is running. Process until the sauce is thickened and then season to taste.

To serve, place the bread slices on a plate, top with the mushrooms and pour over the hollandaise sauce. Serve the soufflés to one side.

READY STEADY COOK Tip
When folding the egg whites into the broccoli mixture, add a tablespoon, then stir in well to loosen the mixture slightly. Fold in the remaining egg whites with a large metal tablespoon, in a figure of eight, being careful not to knock out too much air.

FISH AND SHELLFISH

ROSS BURDEN

LASAGNE FRUTTI DI MARE

Lasagne with seafood in tomato sauce, with avocado sauce and
courgette ribbons
See photograph

Sheila Davies had two favourite dishes — pasta and seafood.
Ross wanted to make her the perfect combination and came up
with this deliciously simple dish.

SERVES 3–4	2 tablespoons chopped fresh basil
5 tomatoes	1 avocado
1 courgette	10 g (½ oz) butter
Juice of 1 lemon	1 tablespoon lime juice
5 tablespoons olive oil	2 tablespoons crème fraiche
1 red onion, chopped	1 tablespoon balsamic vinegar
2 garlic cloves, thinly sliced	Salt and freshly ground black pepper
250 g (9 oz) fresh lasagne sheets	
200 g (7 oz) tub pre-cooked mixed seafood	
(sliced squid, mussels, prawns)	

Score the tomatoes and plunge in boiling water for 1 minute. Drain
and, when cool enough to handle, remove the skins. Cut into quarters
and scoop out the seeds into a sieve placed over a bowl, to catch the
juices. Roughly chop the tomato flesh and set aside.

Top and tail the courgette and then use a potato peeler to slice thinly
lengthways into a large bowl. Add the lemon juice and 2 tablespoons
of olive oil. Season and stir, to coat the courgette. Place a smaller
bowl on top of the courgette slices and fill it with cold water. Leave for
5 minutes; the lemon juice will gently cook the courgette.

Meanwhile, heat a tablespoon of olive oil in a pan over a gentle
heat and add the onion and garlic. Season with pepper and sauté for

5 minutes, until the onion has softened. Set aside to cool.

Cut circles from the lasagne sheets, using a pastry cutter. Bring a pan of salted water to the boil and add a dash of olive oil. Add the pasta and cook for 2–3 minutes, until *al dente*. Drain when cooked.

Meanwhile, add the tomato flesh and reserved juice to the cooled onions and garlic, with a further tablespoon of olive oil. Leave to cook very gently for 5 minutes. Rinse the seafood under running water, drain and add to the pan, with the chopped basil, to heat through for 3 minutes.

Halve the avocado, remove the stone and scoop out the flesh with a large, round spoon. Roughly chop the flesh. Heat the butter in a small pan over a gentle heat and sauté the avocado flesh for a minute on each side, seasoning with pepper. Add the lime juice and crème fraiche and gently shake the pan, to mix.

To serve, put a circle of lasagne on each plate. Layer up lasagne, seafood in tomato sauce and avocado, finishing with pasta. Top with the courgette ribbons and drizzle the plate with the remaining tablespoon of olive oil and the balsamic vinegar.

READY STEADY COOK Tip
Serve this with crusty bread, as there are lots of delicious juices to soak up.

ROSS BURDEN

BRUSCHETTA PESCE

Toasted bread topped with red pepper, with sardines and artichoke

Janette Tovey told us that her husband's favourite hobby was fishing, but if he ever caught anything big enough, she always had problems gutting and preparing the fish. Ross came up with this lovely sardine dish, which shouldn't create too many problems for her.

SERVES 2
Juice of 1 lemon
1 globe artichoke
1 bunch of spring onions
1 red pepper, seeded and quartered
4 slices of bread from a country loaf
1 garlic clove
Olive oil
4 fresh sardines
Seasoned flour, for coating

FOR THE MAYONNAISE
Salt and freshly ground black pepper
2 egg yolks
1 teaspoon caster sugar
1 teaspoon Dijon mustard
2 teaspoons white-wine vinegar
250 ml (9 fl oz) sunflower oil

TO SERVE
1 tablespoon balsamic vinegar
Chervil sprigs, to garnish
Grated zest of 1 lemon

Pre-heat the oven to gas mark 7, 220°C, 425°F. Bring a small pan of water to the boil and add half the lemon juice. To prepare the artichoke bottom, cut or break off the stalk. Using a very sharp knife, carefully cut round the whole artichoke to remove all the outside leaves and discard them. This will leave a cone shape of soft leaves. Trim off any remaining green parts. Cut or snap off the top of the cone and discard, to leave you just the choke bottom. This contains a hairy, inedible centre that is much easier to remove after cooking. Place the artichoke bottom into the boiling water and lemon juice and cook for 8 minutes, or until tender when pierced with a knife, then drain. Leave to cool slightly, then scoop

26

out the inedible centre with a teaspoon and cut the artichoke bottom into quarters.

Cut the green tails off the spring onions and, leaving one end intact, cut into long strips. Put into a bowl of cold water and leave to one side.

Meanwhile, put the pepper quarters on a baking sheet and bake until the skin is blackened.

Heat a griddle pan. Griddle the bread on one side and then turn over. Rub with garlic and drizzle on some olive oil. Remove from the pan.

Heat some olive oil in a large deep frying-pan. To prepare the sardines, cut off the heads and remove the innards. Press them, flesh-side down, on to a board; this will enable the tail and bones to come out in one. Lightly coat the sardines in the flour and fry in the pan for about 2–3 minutes on each side; drain on kitchen paper.

Meanwhile, make the mayonnaise by whisking the egg yolks with a pinch of salt. Add the caster sugar, mustard, vinegar and remaining lemon juice and, whilst continuing to whisk, gradually add the sunflower oil. Season with salt and pepper.

When the skin of the pepper is blackened, leave to steam in a bowl covered with cling film for a couple of minutes. Peel off the skin when it is cool enough to handle.

Arrange the slices of bruschetta, with the red pepper and the artichoke on each plate. Put the sardines on each plate and spoon some of the mayonnaise on to the artichoke. Drizzle some more olive oil and the balsamic vinegar over the peppers and garnish with chervil, lemon zest and the spring-onion tails.

READY STEADY COOK Tip
If you don't fancy preparing globe artichokes, you can buy canned artichoke hearts, which are the pale, tender group of leaves taken from the middle of young artichokes that have not developed hairy, inedible chokes.

ROSS BURDEN

ZUPPA ALLA VONGOLE (CLAM SOUP)

Clams with spaghetti and tomato soup, with sage butter sauce

Coming from a large family, Ena Short was used to cooking in large quantities. Unfortunately, the first meal she cooked for her husband was so huge, the kitchen table collapsed! Ross's substantial soup should keep them all happy.

SERVES 2	1 fennel bulb, cut into small pieces
8 spring onions	1 tablespoon chopped fresh sage
4 tablespoons olive oil	225 g (8 oz) fresh spaghetti
400 g (14 oz) can of chopped tomatoes, drained	290 g (10½ oz) can of clams, drained
1 teaspoon ground turmeric	Salt and freshly ground black pepper
50 g (2 oz) butter	Fresh chives, chervil and basil leaves, to garnish
250 g (9 oz) broccoli, cut into small florets	

Cut the green ends off the spring onions and slice them thinly lengthways. Put into a bowl of cold water and keep to one side. Slice the rest of the spring onions finely. Heat 2 tablespoons of olive oil in a pan and gently fry the spring onions for 2–3 minutes, stirring occasionally, until soft. Then sieve the tomatoes into the pan. Add 150 ml (5 fl oz) of water. Stir and bring to the boil. Add the turmeric and 25 g (1 oz) of butter. Blend with a hand blender, until smooth. Season and keep warm.

Heat 2 tablespoons of olive oil in a shallow pan and fry the broccoli and fennel for 1–2 minutes. Season and drain on kitchen paper. Meanwhile, heat 25 g (1 oz) of butter in a frying-pan and fry the sage for 1 minute until crisp. Bring a pan of salted water to the boil and cook the spaghetti for 3–4 minutes. Drain.

Toss the spaghetti in the sage butter and, using a carving fork or similar, wind a skein of spaghetti and place it in the centre of a soup plate. Arrange the clams and fried vegetables around the pasta and pour the soup over the top. The clams will warm through in the soup. Garnish with the green ends of the spring onions, chives, chervil and basil.

READY STEADY COOK Tip
Spring onion tails go curly when left in cold water, and make a great garnish.

ROSS BURDEN

NINA'S SEAFOOD

Haddock and mussels, with watercress sauce,
Parisienne potatoes and carrot ribbons
See photograph

Canadian Nina Cubrilo told Fern that she'd been in England for a while and was loving it, but there was just one problem. She said that unless she learned to cook at least one dish soon, she would starve to death! Ross thought this colourful seafood dish was a good one to start with.

SERVES 2

FOR THE SAUCE
1 tablespoon olive oil
1 onion, finely chopped
75 g (3 oz) watercress
4 tablespoons white wine
200 ml (7 fl oz) tub of crème fraiche
50 g (2 oz) butter, chilled and diced

FOR THE POTATOES
2 medium potatoes
Vegetable oil, for deep-frying
Salt and freshly ground black pepper

FOR THE FISH
1 haddock fillet
1 tablespoon olive oil
25 g (1 oz) butter
Plain flour, seasoned

FOR THE MUSSELS
4 tablespoons white wine
175 g (6 oz) live mussels
4 carrots
2 tablespoons olive oil
Salt and freshly ground black pepper

Heat the oil in a pan and cook the onion for 4 minutes, until softened. Add the watercress and cook for 3 minutes, until wilted. Add the wine and bring to the boil for a few seconds, then add the crème fraiche and cook for a further two minutes. Put into a food processor and process until smooth. Pass through a sieve into a clean pan and heat through. Just before serving, whisk in the butter, until thick and shiny.

Hollow out the potatoes with a melon baller. Heat the vegetable oil in a pan and fry the potato balls, until golden, crisp and soft in the centre. Drain on kitchen paper. Season.

Score the skin of the haddock. Heat the oil and butter in a frying-pan. Dip the fish in the seasoned flour and fry it skin-side down first for 7–10 minutes, until the skin is crisp and the flesh flakes when tested with a fork. Keep warm.

Heat the wine in a pan and add the mussels. Cover and cook until they open. Discard any of these that do not open. Peel the carrots and cut them into thin ribbons with a potato peeler or mandolin. Heat the olive oil in a pan and cook the carrot ribbons until softened. Season.

Spoon the carrots on to the plate and place the haddock on top. Arrange the mussels on the plate and pour the sauce around. Serve the potatoes separately.

READY STEADY COOK Tip
You could use a deep-fat fryer to fry the potato balls. Fry them for 4 minutes at 190°C/375°F.

ROSS BURDEN

CRESPELLINE AMAZING GRACE

Spinach and prawn pancakes, with piquant sauce and spinach salad

When Fern asked Guide leader Grace Essex why she brought raw prawns along, Grace said that she never normally bought them – because they looked so disgusting! Ross rose to the challenge and cooked up this beautiful dish for her.

SERVES 3–4

FOR THE SPINACH AND PRAWN PANCAKES
250 g (9 oz) spinach, washed
Olive oil for frying
100 g (4 oz) plain flour
Pinch of salt
1 egg
300 ml (10 fl oz) milk
2 tablespoons olive oil
15 g (½ oz) butter
250 g (9 oz) king prawns, peeled and de-veined
150 g (5 oz) goats' cheese
150 ml (5 fl oz) double cream
Salt and freshly ground black pepper

FOR THE COUNTRY SAUCE
1 onion, chopped
Olive oil for frying
2 carrots, grated
Tabasco sauce
2 tablespoons tomato purée
300 ml (10 fl oz) red wine

FOR THE SALAD
1 thin slice of bread, cubed
Olive oil for frying
1 tablespoon white-wine vinegar
4 tablespoons olive oil
Salt and freshly ground black pepper

Pre-heat the oven to gas mark 7, 220°C, 425°F. To make the spinach and prawn pancakes, remove the spinach stalks. Heat a pan with a little olive oil and quickly wilt half the spinach leaves. Mix the flour and salt together and then stir in the egg and milk. Heat the pancake pan with the olive oil and butter. Purée the spinach in a food processor and

31

then mix into the pancake mixture.

Cook the pancakes until golden brown on each side. The mixture should make about 8 pancakes. Cook the prawns until pink on both sides in a small pan with a little olive oil. Remove from the pan and reserve. Season with salt and freshly ground black pepper.

To make the sauce, sauté the onion in a little olive oil for 3 minutes, until soft, using the pan that the prawns were fried in. Add the carrots and cook for 3–4 minutes, until softened. Add a dash of Tabasco sauce, the tomato purée and the red wine, and continue to cook.

Cut up 100 g (4 oz) of the cheese and blend it in a food processor, with the cream. Place a tablespoonful of the mix on the middle of a pancake, with a prawn. Fold into triangles. Repeat with the other pancakes. Arrange the triangles with the point up and the sealed side down in a large ovenproof baking dish. Top with the country sauce and bake for 12 minutes.

Place the remaining spinach leaves in a salad bowl. Fry the bread cubes in a little olive oil until golden and crisp. Make a vinaigrette with the white-wine vinegar and olive oil and season with salt and freshly ground black pepper. Mix in the remaining goats' cheese to a creamy consistency. Dress the salad and sprinkle with the croutons. Serve with the spinach and prawn pancakes and sauce.

READY STEADY COOK Tip
You could add a couple of sticks of celery to the country sauce. String the celery first then slice it into thin slivers and add it with the tomato purée.

Abo
Coco

a
4).

24).
7).

Below: age 55)

ge 75).

Above: Frantic Broccoli and Cheese Soufflés (page 21).
Below: The Star of Christmas (page 10).

Above: My Knees Crumble (page 83).
Below: Vicky's Chocolate Nut Crunch (page 91).

AINSLEY HARRIOTT

HOKI POACHI JOSEPHINE

Hoki roulade stuffed with carrot and leek, with pink fir apple potatoes and fennel sauce

Josie Anderson brought fish along in memory of the most disgusting meal she'd ever had – fish pie cooked by her daughter at school. Ainsley showed her how to cook hoki, which is similar to cod, in the hope that she'd pass on the recipe to her daughter.

SERVES 2	350 g (12 oz) hoki fillet
500 g (1 lb 2 oz) pink fir apple potatoes	1 small fennel bulb, chopped
2 carrots	40 g (1½ oz) butter
1 leek	2 tablespoons double cream
1 tablespoon olive oil	Salt and freshly ground black pepper
150 ml (5 fl oz) white wine	Fresh chives, to garnish
1 tablespoon chopped fresh dill	

Pre-heat the oven to gas mark 7, 220°C, 425°F. Scrub the potatoes and cook whole in boiling, salted water for 10–12 minutes, or until done. Drain, cut into thick slices and keep warm.

Prepare the carrots and leek and cut into matchsticks. Heat the oil and sauté the vegetables for about 3 minutes, to soften. Add 2 tablespoons of the wine, the dill and a little salt and pepper.

Skin the fish fillet and lay it, skinned-side up, on a board. Spread over the vegetables and roll up. Place the fish in a small, ovenproof dish, season and pour over all but 2 tablespoons of the remaining wine. Cover loosely and bake for 15–20 minutes, until the fish is cooked and the flesh flakes easily.

Meanwhile, sauté the fennel in the butter for 2–3 minutes, to soften. Add the 2 tablespoons of wine, the cream and a little seasoning and cook for a further 4–5 minutes, stirring occasionally. Purée the mixture in a blender or food processor, to give a smooth sauce, adding the fish cooking liquor as necessary, to give a pouring consistency. Return to the pan to re-heat; season to taste.

To serve, arrange the sliced potatoes around a hot serving plate and place the fish on top. Pour over the sauce and garnish with the chives, cut into 4 cm (1½ inch) lengths.

AINSLEY HARRIOTT

ROCK OKRA AND FISH CAKES, WITH A COCONUT MALAYSIAN-DAWN SAUCE

White fish cakes with coconut sauce and Thai-spiced okra
See photograph

Dawn Gregory loves cooking, and, together with her two sons,
sings along at the same time using carrots as microphones. Ainsley thought up this delicate,
spicy dish to delight them all.

SERVES 2

FOR THE FISH CAKES
450 g (1 lb) haddock or cod, very finely chopped
2 tablespoons chopped fresh dill
150 g (5 oz) plain flour
1 large egg, beaten
Salt and freshly ground black pepper
3 tablespoons olive oil

FOR THE OKRA
100 g (4 oz) okra
2 tablespoons olive oil

2 lemon grass stalks, chopped
2 lime leaves
2 red chillies, seeded and chopped
1 tablespoon fresh coriander, chopped
1 tablespoon finely chopped onion

FOR THE SAUCE
100 g (4 oz) creamed coconut, grated
150 ml (5 fl oz) milk
1 tablespoon chopped fresh coriander
1 teaspoon cayenne pepper
Salt and freshly ground black pepper

34

Mix together the fish, dill, 40 g (1½ oz) of the flour, egg and seasoning in a bowl. Making sure your hands are well-floured, take handfuls of the mixture and shape into 5 cm (2 inch) patties (it should make 12). Coat each patty with more flour.

Heat the oil in a frying-pan. When hot, fry the cakes for 4–5 minutes each side until golden. Drain on absorbent kitchen paper and keep warm.

Put the okra in a pan of water and bring to the boil. Once the water is boiling, drain the okra and cut them in half lengthways.

Heat the oil in a small frying-pan. Add the spices, reserving half the chilli, the okra and onion. Cook for 4–5 minutes.

For the sauce, melt the coconut in a pan, with the milk and the rest of the chilli. Add the coriander and cayenne pepper and season. Cook on a low heat for 5 minutes, until the coconut has melted; add more water if it seems too thick.

To serve, place the fish cakes in a line along one side of the plate. Put the okra along the other side and pour the sauce over the fish cakes.

READY STEADY COOK Tips
If you can't buy chopped fish ready-prepared,
mince or process your own from skinned white-fish fillets.

Sunflower, vegetable or groundnut oil could be used
as alternatives to olive oil.

AINSLEY HARRIOTT

SWEET CAROLINE'S CALAMITY MACKEREL

Mackerel with chilli, herbs and lemon, with sautéd sweet potato

Caroline Virgo admitted that she taught herself to cook after leaving home – not just for survival but mainly to impress boyfriends – so Ainsley devised this irresistible and flavourful mackerel dish for her.

SERVES 2	Grated zest and juice of 1 lemon
3 spring onions, to garnish	2 tablespoons finely chopped fresh coriander
1 sprig of fresh coriander	1 tablespoon finely chopped fresh parsley
225 g (8 oz) sweet potato, peeled and sliced	1 teaspoon finely chopped fresh mint
lengthways	1 teaspoon finely chopped fresh basil
4 tablespoons olive oil	1 teaspoon finely chopped fresh tarragon
2 whole mackerel, cleaned and scaled	2 garlic cloves, finely chopped
6 fresh red chillies, 4 seeded and chopped,	½ iceberg lettuce, finely shredded
2 seeded and sliced, to garnish	Salt and freshly ground black pepper

Slit the ends of the spring onions lengthways, without cutting them right through, and put them in iced water until the ends curl. Bring some water to the boil and season with salt. Add the sprig of coriander and the sweet potato and cook for 6–8 minutes, to soften. Remove the sweet potato and pat dry with kitchen paper (discard the coriander). Heat 2 tablespoons of oil in a frying-pan and fry the sweet potato for 2–3 minutes on each side, until browned.

Cut four diagonal slits, 1 cm (½ inch) deep in each side of the mackerel. Put the chopped chilli in a bowl, add the lemon zest and juice, chopped herbs and garlic and season. Mix all the ingredients together and stuff three-quarters into the fish.

Heat 2 tablespoons of oil in a shallow pan. Add the mackerel, cover and cook for 6 minutes, turning halfway through. Then transfer to the grill to brown well on both sides.

Mix the lettuce with the remaining herb mixture.

To serve, heap a bed of lettuce on a plate, add a layer of sweet potato, sit the mackerel on top and pour the cooking juices over. Garnish with the spring onions and sliced chillies.

AINSLEY HARRIOTT

FIERY-FARING SALMON

Salmon fillet with watercress salad and citrus and sage mushrooms
See photograph

Whilst chopping, Paula Atkins told Ainsley that her favourite pastime is tracing her family tree and taking photographs of gravestones, which astonishes her local photo developer. Paula was delighted with this simple salmon dish.

SERVES 2	2 salmon fillets or steaks
175 g (6 oz) tagliatelle	100 g (4 oz) chestnut mushrooms, thickly sliced
3 tablespoons olive oil	1 tablespoon finely chopped fresh sage
1 onion, finely chopped	2 tablespoons lemon juice or lime juice
75 ml (3 fl oz) white wine	75 g (3 oz) watercress, chopped
150 ml (5 fl oz) double cream	2 red peppers, seeded and thinly sliced
1 teaspoon saffron strands	salt and freshly ground black pepper

Cook the pasta, as instructed on the packet.

Heat a tablespoon of the oil and fry the onion for 4 minutes, until soft. Add the wine and cook for 4 minutes, until the liquid has reduced by a third. Then stir in the cream and cook for 1–2 minutes, until the sauce begins to thicken. Stir in the saffron.

When the pasta is *al dente*, drain it. Pour the sauce over the drained pasta and mix thoroughly. Keep warm.

Brush the salmon steaks with oil, season and cook on a ridged griddle or in a non-stick frying-pan for 7–8 minutes, turning halfway through. Put the mushrooms in a pan with a tablespoon of oil, cover and cook for 2 minutes. Add the sage and half the lemon or lime juice, then cover and cook for another 2–3 minutes, until the mushrooms are soft.

Mix the watercress, peppers, one tablespoon of olive oil and remaining lemon or lime juice together and season.

To serve, arrange the watercress and peppers around the edge of a large serving dish. Using a large carving fork or similar, wind up the tagliatelle and drop into the centre to make nests. Top with the salmon and serve with the mushrooms.

READY STEADY COOK Tip
If you have a griddle pan, make sure it is thoroughly pre-heated before use to prevent the salmon sticking.

A I N S L E Y   H A R R I O T T

A LOAD OF OLD SCALLOPS

Scallops and caramelized shallots, in pastry cases, with potato nests filled with cabbage

On this special Christmas show, *Birds of a Feather* star, Pauline Quirke, admitted that she hated all vegetables except for processed peas, but became a complete convert to cabbage after tasting Ainsley's efforts.

SERVES 2

2 medium potatoes	1 tablespoon demerara sugar
150 g (5 oz) butter	225 g (8 oz) scallops
1 egg yolk	4 tablespoons white wine
350 g (12 oz) puff pastry	150 ml (5 fl oz) double cream
1 egg, lightly beaten	¼ Savoy cabbage, shredded
1 tablespoon olive oil	1 tablespoon soy sauce
8 shallots, 6 left whole, 2 thinly sliced	1 tablespoon clear honey
	Salt and freshly ground black pepper

Pre-heat the oven to gas mark 7, 220°C, 425°F. Cut the potatoes into chunks and cook in boiling, salted water for 12–15 minutes until soft. Drain and mash until smooth with 50 g (2 oz) of the butter, the egg yolk and salt and pepper. Put the potato into a piping bag, pipe nest shapes on to a greased baking sheet, and bake for 10 minutes, until golden.

Meanwhile, roll out the pastry and, using a 20 cm (8 inch) plate, cut out four discs. Keep two to one side for the base and then, with a 15 cm (6 inch) plate, take out the centre of two of the discs so you are left with a ring. Discard the centre piece of pastry. Brush the bases with egg and place a ring on top of each base. Brush with more egg. Place on a greased baking sheet and bake until golden and risen.

Heat the olive oil and 25 g (1 oz) of the butter in a pan and fry the whole shallots, until softened and turning golden. Then add the demerara sugar and leave them to caramelize. Meanwhile, in a separate pan, heat 25 g (1 oz) of the butter and cook the sliced shallots, until softened. Then add the scallops and cook for a further 2 minutes, stirring occasionally. Remove the scallops and keep to one side. Pour in the white wine and reduce by half. Then add the double cream and heat through. Before serving, return the scallops to the pan and warm through.

Heat 25 g (1 oz) of butter in a pan and fry the cabbage for 2 minutes. Then add the soy sauce and honey. Stir together well.

To serve, put the scallops into the pastry cases, with the caramelized shallots. Put the cabbage into the potato cases, using a slotted spoon.

READY STEADY COOK Tips
You could buy a 500 g (1¼ lb) packet of ready-to-roll fresh puff pastry and freeze any remainder.

Try to get a mixture of large and small scallops, if possible. The larger scallops will need to be cooked for 1 minute before adding the smaller scallops and cooking for a further minute.

POULTRY AND GAME

ROSS BURDEN

POLLO BUCCO

Savoy cabbage 'basket' filled with saffron risotto and chicken kebabs

Animal-mad Joanne Carroll works as a nurse so finds little time for cooking. She has four dogs, including a three-legged dog called Peg Leg, who was rescued from under a bush in Liverpool. Ross cooked up this tasty chicken dish that she can prepare after work.

SERVES 4	5 tablespoons olive oil
1 Savoy cabbage	Juice of 1 lemon
25 g (1 oz) butter	150 g (5 oz) button mushrooms
1 onion, finely chopped	1 large red pepper, seeded and cut
2 chicken stock cubes	into bite-sized pieces
250 ml (9 fl oz) white wine	Finely grated zest of 1 orange
225 g (8 oz) arborio risotto rice	2 tablespoons finely chopped fresh parsley
10–15 saffron strands	3 garlic cloves, crushed
2 skinless, boneless chicken breasts	Salt and freshly ground black pepper

Remove any damaged outer leaves from the cabbage, gently fold back the remaining outer leaves and cut out the middle, so you are left with a cabbage 'basket'. Place the cabbage basket in a pan quarter-filled with boiling water and cook for 10 minutes, until tender. Drain and refresh under cold water.

Meanwhile, melt the butter in a separate pan, add the onion and gently sauté for 3–4 minutes, until soft. Bring 1.2 litres (2 pints) of water to the boil in a separate pan and add the stock cubes and 150 ml (5 fl oz) of wine; keep this stock just simmering. Add the rice to the softened onion and stir to coat in the butter. Pour in two ladles of the hot stock, add the saffron and stir gently. Leave to simmer gently and, when the stock has been absorbed, add a further two ladles of hot stock; stir and leave to simmer again. Continue this process until the rice is tender – about 20 minutes.

Slice the chicken breasts into 2 cm (¾ inch) pieces and put into a bowl with 3 tablespoons of the olive oil and the lemon juice. Stir to coat and set to one side for 5 minutes, to marinate. Heat a griddle pan over a high heat. Thread four kebab skewers with the chicken, mushrooms and pepper pieces and season well. Place the kebabs on the griddle and cook for 2 minutes before turning. Cook for a further 2 minutes and turn again. Repeat this process until the chicken is a rich, golden colour and is cooked. Just before the end of cooking, sprinkle the remaining wine over the chicken, so its flavour is absorbed, and season again.

Shred the uncooked cabbage finely. Heat the remaining 2 tablespoons of olive oil in a wok over a high heat and add the cabbage. Stir-fry until the cabbage has wilted and is cooked.

In a separate bowl, mix together the orange zest, 1 tablespoon of chopped fresh parsley and the crushed garlic.

To serve, place the steamed cabbage basket in a deep serving bowl. Fill the bottom with the shredded cabbage, pile the risotto on top and then add the kebabs. Sprinkle over the orange, parsley and garlic mixture and top with the remaining tablespoon of chopped parsley.

READY STEADY COOK Tip
If you don't have a griddle pan, use a non-stick frying-pan instead.

R O S S   B U R D E N

FEGATINI RUAPEHU

Chicken liver bruschetta with lentil sauce, green beans and fried sage leaves

Ross was more than happy to cook for fellow New Zealander Philip Morris who described his cooking as 'boogie cuisine' – the two most essential ingredients being music and a bottle of wine!

SERVES 2	Large handful of fresh mint leaves
7 tablespoons olive oil	Large handful of fresh flatleaf parsley
4 medium-sized carrots, diced	75 g (3 oz) fine green beans, topped and tailed
3 celery sticks, diced	12 sage leaves
1 shallot, finely chopped	4 slices of white country-style bread
420 g (14 oz) can of green lentils, drained	400 g (14 oz) fresh chicken livers
Juice of ½ lemon	1 tablespoon balsamic vinegar
1 teaspoon ground cumin	Salt and freshly ground black pepper
1 tablespoon chopped fresh mint	

Put 4 tablespoons of oil in a deep frying-pan. Add the carrots, celery and shallot and cook for 5 minutes, until soft, stirring occasionally. Add the lentils, lemon juice, cumin, salt and pepper and mint and mix together. Put the mint leaves and flatleaf parsley in a food processor and process for 30 seconds. Stir into the lentils. Keep to one side.

Bring a pan of water to the boil and blanch the beans for 1–2 minutes. Drain, refresh in cold running water and keep to one side.

In the same pan, heat a tablespoon of olive oil. Fry the sage leaves for 30 seconds. Drain on kitchen paper and keep to one side.

Cut four discs out of the bread for the bruschetta. Heat a griddle pan brushed lightly with a tablespoon of oil and fry the bread on both sides, until golden. Heat a shallow frying-pan with a tablespoon of oil. When hot, fry the chicken livers for 2–3 minutes on each side, until browned. Remove from the pan and keep to one side. Deglaze the pan with the balsamic vinegar. Return the chicken livers to the pan and leave off the heat.

To serve, put a piece of bruschetta on a plate, top with the chicken livers and repeat. Serve the beans and lentils on either side. Garnish with the sage leaves.

R O S S   B U R D E N

HIT-THE-FLOOR QUAIL

Braised quail with cream sauce, sautéd aubergine and green-bean gratin

Canadian Jane Neisler wanted Ross to create something a little romantic for her boyfriend as the last time she cooked him a candlelit meal, she leant across the table to give him a kiss and set her hair on fire.

SERVES 2

4 tablespoons olive oil
4 quails
100 g (4 oz) green grapes
175 ml (6 fl oz) white wine
1 aubergine, roughly chopped
2 slices of white country-style bread
2 garlic cloves, finely chopped
100 g (4 oz) green beans, topped and tailed
1 small onion, finely chopped
1 teaspoon saffron strands
50 ml (2 fl oz) double cream
420 g (14 oz) can of butter beans, drained
Salt and freshly ground black pepper

FOR THE MAYONNAISE

2 egg yolks
1 tablespoon white-wine vinegar
1 teaspoon saffron strands
1 teaspoon sugar
1 teaspoon French mustard
300 ml (10 fl oz) sunflower oil
Salt and freshly ground black pepper
1 lemon, halved and flesh scooped out, to serve (optional)

44

Pre-heat the oven to gas mark 6, 200°C, 400°F. Heat a flameproof casserole dish with a tablespoon of oil. Brown the quails all over. Then add the grapes and 75 ml (3 fl oz) of white wine. Cover with a lid and bring to the boil and then reduce the heat to a simmer and cook for 15–20 minutes. Top up the quails during cooking, if necessary.

Meanwhile, put the aubergine pieces in a sieve or colander, sprinkle over a tablespoon of salt and leave to stand, to allow the liquid from the aubergine to drain. This will take about 10 minutes.

In a food processor, process the bread for 30 seconds. Add a tablespoon of oil and a garlic clove. Process again for 20 seconds and set aside. Blanch the beans in boiling water for 2 minutes. Drain and put into an ovenproof dish. Cover with the breadcrumb mixture and cook in the oven for 10–12 minutes until golden and crisp on top.

Heat a tablespoon of olive oil in a pan and fry the onion for 5 minutes, or until softened, stirring occasionally. Add the other garlic clove and fry for a further minute. Season and then add the remaining wine, the saffron and the cream. Bring to the boil, reduce the heat and add the butter beans; then leave to simmer over a gentle heat.

To make the mayonnaise, put all the ingredients, except the oil, in a food processor or bowl and mix together. Then slowly add the sunflower oil, processing continuously until thick and creamy. Season and leave to one side. Heat a tablespoon of oil in a frying-pan and, when it is very hot, fry the aubergine pieces until golden.

Put the quails and grapes on to serving plates and arrange the aubergine around the plates. Pour the cream sauce over the quails. Serve the green beans separately and serve the mayonnaise in 2 scooped-out halves of a lemon or a small dish.

ROSS BURDEN

OSTRICH IN TIME FOR £4.99

Ostrich steak in piquant sauce, potato galettes and stuffed mushrooms

Social worker Sue Riley thought New Zealander Ross was the perfect chef to show her what on earth to do with ostrich. She told Fern that her husband eats absolutely anything, but ostrich was something he'd never tried.

SERVES 2	3 flat mushrooms
1 Savoy cabbage, 6 large outer leaves only	2 red-skinned potatoes, thinly sliced
2 carrots, cut into ribbons	100 ml (3½ fl oz) red wine
3½ tablespoons olive oil	Vegetable stock cube
175 g (6 oz) ostrich steak	1 tablespoon balsamic vinegar
1 onion, finely chopped	1 teaspoon brown sugar
3 slices of white country-style bread	Salt and freshly ground black pepper
2 tablespoons chopped fresh tarragon	Sprigs of fresh flatleaf parsley to garnish

Pre-heat the oven to gas mark 6, 200°C, 400°F. Bring a large pan of water to the boil. Blanch the cabbage leaves for 2 minutes and the carrot ribbons for a further minute. Drain and refresh in cold water and set aside. Heat a tablespoon of olive oil in a frying-pan and brown the ostrich steak on all sides. Remove from the pan and wrap the carrot ribbons and then the cabbage leaves around the steak. Secure with cocktail sticks, put on to a baking sheet and bake for 10 minutes. For a well-done steak, cook for 15 minutes.

In the same frying-pan used to fry the ostrich, fry the onion for 3–4 minutes, stirring occasionally. Meanwhile, in a food processor, process the bread for 10 seconds. In a bowl, put the breadcrumbs, tarragon, half the cooked onion and ½ tablespoon of olive oil. Season and mix together. Remove the stalks and put the mushrooms upturned on a baking sheet. Divide the breadcrumb mixture between them. Bake for 8–10 minutes.

Heat the last 2 tablespoons of olive oil in a small pan. Shape the sliced potatoes into galettes, by overlapping them to make two circular discs. Fry on both sides for 2–3 minutes, until golden. Pour the red wine over the remaining onion and add the vegetable stock cube. Stir in the vinegar and the sugar. Season and cook for a further 2–3 minutes, stirring to dissolve the stock cube. Sieve the sauce and keep warm.

To serve, flood the base of a plate with the sauce and put a potato galette in the centre. Cut the ostrich in half, remove the cocktail sticks and place on the potato galette. Serve the stuffed mushrooms separately and garnish both plates with flatleaf parsley.

READY STEADY COOK Tips
Use a potato peeler to cut the carrots into ribbons.

You may wish to use two ostrich steaks and serve one steak per person. The recipe is quite rich and gamey, and one steak halved between two will be delicious, but if you're both feeling extra hungry, opt for one steak each.

Ostrich steak is best served rare, but you can increase the cooking time by five minutes if you prefer well-done meat, although cooking for too long will dry it out.

ROSS BURDEN

TACCHINO ALLA SENESE

Turkey steaks with cream and bacon sauce, with watercress
and rice timbales
See photograph

Francesca Parkes met her husband at work. Their eyes met across a crowded room — and what do
they do? They're both opticians! Ross created this visually stunning dish to impress them both.

SERVES 2	100 ml (4 fl oz) white wine
1 chicken stock cube	150 ml (5 fl oz) double cream
175 g (6 oz) long-grain rice	5 black olives, pitted and halved
75 g (3 oz) watercress	Butter
1 tablespoon olive oil	1 beef tomato skinned, seeded and chopped into
2 x 150 g (5 oz) turkey steaks	1 cm (½ inch) pieces
120 g (4½ oz) pancetta, cubed	Salt and freshly ground black pepper
1 onion, finely chopped	

Bring a pan of water to the boil and stir in the stock cube. Add the
rice. Cover and simmer gently for 10–12 minutes or until the rice is
soft. Meanwhile, take the watercress leaves off the stalks and blanch
them in boiling water for 10 seconds. Drain and keep to one side.

Heat the olive oil in a frying-pan and fry the turkey steaks for 5–6
minutes on each side. Fry the pancetta and onion in a dry frying-pan for
5 minutes, stirring occasionally. Then add the white wine and reduce for
20 seconds. Add the cream and boil for a minute. When the turkey is
cooked, put it into the sauce and stir in the olives. Season.

Drain the rice when it is cooked. Put a small piece of butter in the
bottom of two ramekins or cups. Put a layer of watercress on the base
of each. Then half fill with rice, and another layer of watercress and
then fill to the top with rice. Press down firmly.

To serve, turn out the timbales on a plate. Put the turkey steaks on the
plate and pour over the sauce. Garnish with the tomato pieces.

POULTRY AND GAME

AINSLEY HARRIOTT

TWANGY LITTLE FAT DUCK

Marinated duck slices with mango sauce and minty,
lemony green beans

A fast-food freak, Jane Milner wanted Ainsley to show her how to cook at least one dish in the vain attempt to get herself a husband.

SERVES 2	150 ml (5 fl oz) white wine
2 x 350 g (12 oz) boneless duck breasts	1 mango, peeled, stoned and sliced
3 tablespoons olive oil	5 cardamom pods, bruised
1 tablespoon sesame oil	15 g (½ oz) butter
2 tablespoons soy sauce	1 garlic clove, finely chopped
1 tablespoon clear honey	1 tablespoon chopped fresh mint
2.5 cm (1 inch) piece of fresh root ginger, finely chopped	1 teaspoon grated lemon zest
	Salt and freshly ground black pepper
1 teaspoon dried oregano	Spring onion tassels and sprigs of fresh mint, to garnish
5 spring onions, sliced diagonally	
225 g (8 oz) green beans, trimmed	

Trim half the skin and fat off the duck breast. Cut the duck breast into thin slices and put in a bowl with a tablespoon of olive oil, the sesame oil, soy sauce, honey, ginger, oregano, spring onions and seasoning. Mix together well and set aside, to marinate.

Cook the green beans in a pan of boiling water for 2 minutes. Drain and refresh under cold running water.

Put the wine in a small pan, bring to the boil and simmer for a minute. Add the sliced mango and cardamom pods and simmer for 3 minutes. Remove and discard the cardamom pods. Put the mango sauce in a food processor and whizz until smooth.

Heat a tablespoon of olive oil in a frying-pan, until very hot. Add the strips of duck and the marinade and cook for 4 minutes, until browned, stirring occasionally.

Melt the butter and a tablespoon of olive oil in a pan, add the garlic and cook for a minute. Add the chopped mint, lemon zest and green beans and cook, stirring, for 1–2 minutes.

Pile the green beans on serving plates and top with the strips of duck, using a slotted spoon. Spoon the mango sauce around the edge and garnish with spring onion tassels, sprigs of mint and the scored mango skin (see below), if you like.

READY STEADY COOK Tips
If you like, slice a piece of mango skin with a thin layer of flesh attached, score in a lattice and push the skin up. Reserve for garnish.

Try to buy duck breasts with the skin left on. This adds richness and taste and prevents them from drying out during frying.

AINSLEY HARRIOTT

MAMMA MIA, WICKED CHICKEN, RICE AND PEAS

Spicy chicken with rice and kidney beans

Italian Sergio Dogliani wanted Ainsley to invent something he could cook for his beautiful wife Emma that was delightful, delicious but NOT ITALIAN!! Although his Italian cooking is excellent, it was getting *basta, basta.*

SERVES 2–3	200 ml (7 fl oz) carton of cocunut cream
2 corn-fed chicken leg portions	2 tablespoons sunflower oil
Juice of ½ lemon	1 onion, chopped
1 chicken stock cube	1 green pepper, sliced

2 tablespoons curry powder

1 tablespoon paprika

2 sprigs of fresh thyme

1 green chilli, seeded and thinly sliced

400 g (14 oz) can of chopped tomatoes

50 g (2 oz) butter

2 garlic cloves, crushed

100 g (4 oz) long-grain rice

200 g (7 oz) can of red kidney beans

Lemon slices, to garnish

Chop the chicken into chunks with a large, sharp knife. Put into a bowl, with the lemon juice, and turn to coat evenly. Rinse the chicken in cold water and pat dry.

In a large measuring jug, dissolve the chicken stock cube in 300 ml (10 fl oz) of boiling water. Add the coconut cream and mix the two together.

Heat the oil in a deep frying-pan, add the onion and most of the green pepper, reserving a little for garnish. Cook to soften and then add the chicken pieces and brown on all sides. Add the curry powder, paprika, 1 sprig of thyme and two-thirds of the chilli, or to taste. Add the tomatoes and 120 ml (4 fl oz) of the coconut-stock mixture and bring to the boil then simmer, stirring occasionally, for 15–20 minutes, until the chicken is cooked through.

Meanwhile, melt the butter in another pan, add the garlic and rice and cook for 1–2 minutes. Add the beans and their juice and the remaining sprig of thyme. Add half the coconut-stock mixture, bring to the boil and cook for 12–15 minutes, until the rice is tender, adding more of the liquid as it is absorbed.

Serve the chicken with the rice and garnish with the reserved pepper slices and lemon slices on the side of the plate. Use the remaining chilli to garnish.

READY STEADY COOK Tip
You could use 200 ml (7 fl oz) of coconut milk if you prefer, or use 55 g (2 oz) of creamed coconut made up to 200 ml with boiling water.

IAN'S CHICKEN STUFFETA

Chicken and feta cheese vine-leaf parcels,
with tomato sauce and rice timbales
See photograph

Ian Draper works for a Greek travel company during the summer and admitted that during the
winter he dances in a Greek dance troupe called Marcus and Spencus!

SERVES 2

FOR THE VINE-LEAF PARCELS
150 g (5 oz) rice
2 chicken breasts, cut into 9 strips
175 g (6 oz) feta cheese, cubed into 18
9 preserved vine leaves
2 tablespoons olive oil
Salt and freshly ground black pepper

FOR THE SAUCE
3 tablespoons olive oil
3 spring onions, sliced
2 garlic cloves, chopped
6 tomatoes, skinned, seeded and finely sliced
3 tablespoons white wine
Salt and freshly ground black pepper
6 black stoned olives, sliced, to garnish

Cook the rice according to the instructions on the packet. When cooked, put the rice into two buttered ramekins or cups.

Wrap a piece of chicken and cube of feta cheese in a vine leaf, turning in the ends to make a parcel. Season and thread on a skewer (three stuffed vine leaves per skewer). Fry the vine-leaf parcels in 1 tablespoon of olive oil for 5 minutes; then sprinkle with the remaining tablespoon of olive oil and finish cooking under a hot grill for a further 15–20 minutes, turning occasionally until the chicken is cooked.

To make the sauce, heat 3 tablespoons of olive oil. Add the spring onions and garlic and fry for 1 minute. Add the tomatoes and wine, cover and bring to the boil. Then leave to simmer for 10–12 minutes, until the sauce has reduced to a fairly thick consistency. Season to taste.

To serve, turn the rice out on to a plate. Spoon the tomato sauce on to one side of the plate and place the chicken vine leaves on top of the sauce. Garnish with the olive slices.

READY STEADY COOK Tips

Soak wooden skewers in water for 20 minutes before using,
otherwise they will char. Alternatively, use metal skewers.

Fresh vine leaves should be blanched in boiling water for
3 minutes before use. Vine leaves sold in brine should be drained
and left to soak in boiling water for 20–30 minutes then rinsed
and dried on kitchen paper, to remove saltiness.

A I N S L E Y   H A R R I O T T

CHICKEN AND GREEN POTATO CAKE

Spinach and potato cake with spicy, marinated chicken chunks

Student Mark Tarchetti's plea to Ainsley was to cook him something edible.
The canteen at Durham University is, according to Mark, dreadful and serves mash and
cabbage with everything. Putting together ingredients for less than a fiver was no problem –
he's studying economics.

SERVES 2

2 chicken breasts or quarters, skinned, trimmed and cut into chunks
1 teaspoon garam masala
½ teaspoon ground turmeric
1 teaspoon ground coriander
½ teaspoon cayenne pepper
1 teaspoon ground ginger
1 tablespoon chopped fresh coriander
Grated zest of ½ lemon

5 tablespoons olive oil
2 large potatoes, very thinly sliced
1 onion, ½ cut into rings, ½ chopped
2 garlic cloves, chopped
1 teaspoon ground cumin
225 g (8 oz) frozen spinach leaves
2 tomatoes, sliced
Salt and freshly ground black pepper
Fresh parsley and lemon wedges, to garnish

Mix together the chicken chunks, garam masala, turmeric, ground coriander, cayenne pepper, ginger, fresh coriander, lemon zest and a tablespoon of olive oil. Ensure that the chicken is completely coated and leave to marinate for 5 minutes (ideally, the chicken should marinate overnight).

Microwave the potato slices on full power for 8 minutes with 5 tablespoons of water. Drain under cold water to separate as they tend to stick together.

Sauté the chopped onions and garlic in a tablespoon of oil for 2–3 minutes, until soft. Add the cumin and the spinach. Season, cover and cook for 3–4 minutes.

Heat a tablespoon of oil and sauté the marinated chicken in a pan for about 10 minutes, stirring occasionally, until the chicken is completely cooked.

Heat 2 tablespoons of olive oil in a frying-pan. Place half the potato slices on the base of the pan, to make a thin layer. Season and then spoon the spinach on top. Place the tomato slices on top of the spinach and cover with the remaining potato slices. Place under a hot grill for 5 minutes, until the potatoes have turned golden brown.

To serve, carefully turn the spinach and potato cake out on to a plate. Spoon the chicken over the top and garnish with the raw onion rings and a little fresh parsley and lemon.

READY STEADY COOK Tip
You could use chicken breasts, instead of chicken quarters, to save trimming and boning.

AINSLEY HARRIOTT

ON THE GAME, WITH ALAN AND AINS

Wood-pigeon breasts with raspberry sauce, with green beans, sliced potatoes and avocado with raspberry dressing
See photograph

Alan Cavanagh said he wanted to come on the show so 'I'll have something to bore my children with and, more importantly, have something to talk about from my park bench come my twilight years ... '

SERVES 2

FOR THE AVOCADO WITH RASPBERRY DRESSING
1 tablespoon red-wine vinegar
3 tablespoons olive oil
Juice of ½ orange
100 g (4 oz) frozen raspberries, thawed
1 avocado
½ orange, peeled and cut into segments
Grated zest of 1 orange
50 g (2 oz) frozen raspberries, thawed, to decorate

FOR THE PIGEON BREASTS
1 wood pigeon
Grated zest and juice of 1 orange
1 shallot, chopped
1 garlic clove
1 bay leaf
300 ml (10 fl oz) red wine

FOR THE SAUCE
50 g (2 oz) butter
3 shallots, thinly sliced
50 g (2 oz) frozen raspberries, thawed
Salt and freshly ground black pepper

FOR THE VEGETABLES
100 g (4 oz) new potatoes
2 tablespoons olive oil
1 tablespoon sesame oil
100 g (4 oz) green beans, trimmings reserved
Salt and freshly ground black pepper

To make the dressing for the avocado, in a blender or using a whisk, blend the vinegar, oil, orange juice and 100 g (4 oz) of the raspberries. Keep to one side. Cut the avocado in half, remove the stone and peel. Then make a fan by cutting slices 5 mm (¼ inch) from the thin end to the bottom. Fan out on a plate. Arrange the orange segments amongst the avocado slices. Decorate with orange zest and the remaining raspberries and pour over the dressing. Keep to one side.

Remove the breasts from the wood pigeon. Coat the breasts in the orange zest and set aside, to marinate. Put the pigeon bones, shallot, garlic, bay leaf, green bean trimmings, 150 ml (5 fl oz) of the wine and half the orange juice in a large pan. Bring to the boil and then reduce the heat and leave to simmer.

Heat 25 g (1 oz) of the butter in a pan and fry the shallots, until softened. Add the raspberries, remaining wine and 150 ml (5 fl oz) of strained stock. Bring to the boil and leave to reduce by half. Blend with a hand blender then sieve to remove the pips. Season and whisk in the remaining butter, cut in cubes.

Bring a pan of water to the boil and cook the potatoes, until soft. Drain. Toss in a tablespoon of olive oil. Slice thinly and keep warm.

Heat the remaining oil in a pan and fry the wood-pigeon breasts for a minute on each side. Transfer to a baking dish and roast for 6 minutes.

Meanwhile heat the sesame oil in a frying-pan and sauté the beans for 4–5 minutes. Add the remaining orange juice and season to taste.

To serve, put the potato slices and beans in the centre of the plate. Put the pigeon breasts on top and pour the sauce around the plate. Serve with the avocado with raspberry dressing.

READY STEADY COOK Tip
You could serve the avocado with raspberry dressing with crusty bread separately as a starter, if preferred.

FRANK'S DUCK FANCY

Smoked duck breast with lentils, with spicy red cabbage, potato cakes and carrot and orange salad

Fern asked Frank how good his cooking was. 'Just good enough to keep someone alive,' he replied. Ainsley thought this simple duck dish would inspire Frank's cooking to greater heights.

SERVES 2

FOR THE LENTILS

1 tablespoon olive oil
1 onion, chopped
1 garlic clove, chopped
1 teaspoon ground cumin
1 teaspoon ground cinnamon
1 teaspoon paprika
300 g (11 oz) can of Puy lentils, drained
1 tablespoon tomato purée
½ tablespoon chopped fresh rosemary
1 vegetable stock cube
1 smoked duck breast

FOR THE CABBAGE

1 baby red cabbage, shredded
150 ml (5 fl oz) red wine

Pinch of ground cumin

FOR THE POTATO CAKES

2 medium potatoes, coarsely grated
1 tablespoon olive oil
Salt and freshly ground black pepper

FOR THE SALAD

1 tablespoon olive oil
Juice of ½ orange
1 teaspoon poppy seeds
1 tablespoon white-wine vinegar
4 carrots, cut into matchsticks
2 oranges, sliced
Salt and freshly ground black pepper
1 tablespoon chopped fresh coriander

Heat a tablespoon of oil in a pan and fry the onion and garlic, with the cumin, cinnamon and paprika for 3–4 minutes, until soft. Add the lentils, tomato purée, rosemary, stock cube and 2 tablespoons of boiling water. Take the skin off the duck breast and set it aside. Cut half the duck breast into small pieces and stir into the lentils.

In a separate pan, cover the cabbage and red wine and cook gently, with a pinch of cumin, for 12–15 minutes, until the cabbage is soft.

Squeeze the excess liquid out of the potatoes and season. Heat the oil in a pan and form four potato cakes. Fry for 10–12 minutes, turning halfway through cooking, until golden on both sides. Drain on kitchen paper. Put them on a plate and spoon the re-heated lentils and cabbage on top.

Heat the remaining olive oil in a pan. Cut the duck skin into small pieces and fry for 2–3 minutes, until crisp. Drain on kitchen paper.

Meanwhile, mix together the orange juice, poppy seeds and vinegar and season. Arrange the carrot and orange slices on a plate. Cut the other half of the duck into thin strips and put them on top of the carrots. Drizzle over the dressing and garnish with coriander and the crisp duck skin.

ROSS BURDEN

TURKEY TRICOLORE

Poached turkey breasts with cranberry chutney, with orange-topped broccoli and mashed potatoes
See photograph

Pam wanted Ross to create a romantic but low-fat meal to cook for her husband, despite the fact that he is hardly Mr Romantic himself. He proposed to Pam at a football match!

SERVES 2

FOR THE CHUTNEY
1 onion, chopped
225 g (8 oz) cranberries, fresh or frozen, thawed if frozen
100 g (4 oz) soft light brown sugar
½ teaspoon ground cumin
½ teaspoon ground cloves
½ teaspoon ground black pepper
150 ml (5 fl oz) white-wine vinegar

FOR THE TURKEY
175 g (6 oz) turkey breast fillets
300 ml (10 fl oz) rosé wine
6 whole peppercorns
2 bay leaves

FOR THE VEGETABLES
350 g (12 oz) potatoes, peeled and cut in 1 cm (½ inch) cubes
225 g (8 oz) broccoli, cut in two pieces

58

2 tablespoons low-fat natural yoghurt	Salt and freshly ground black pepper
2 tablespoons chopped fresh basil	Sprigs of fresh basil, to garnish
1 orange	

Put the onion, cranberries, sugar, cumin, cloves, pepper and white-wine vinegar in a pan and bring to the boil. Reduce the heat and simmer for 7–8 minutes. Lightly mash with a potato masher and then continue to simmer, until the sauce is syrupy.

Meanwhile, cut horizontally three-quarters of the way through each turkey breast and then open out in a butterfly shape. Put in a large frying-pan with the wine, peppercorns and bay leaves and poach for 10 minutes, until cooked through.

Cook the potatoes in a pan of boiling water for 8 minutes, until tender. Cook the broccoli in a pan of boiling water for 6 minutes. Drain the potatoes and then mash with the yoghurt, chopped basil and seasoning.

Cut a few needleshreds of the orange zest, using a zester. Cut half of the orange into segments and squeeze the juice from the other half. Pile the mashed potatoes on to serving plates and serve with the poached turkey, the broccoli topped with orange segments, needleshreds and juice and the cranberry chutney.

Garnish with fresh basil and the bay leaves.

READY STEADY COOK Tip
Any left-over cranberry chutney can be stored in an airtight container in the fridge for up to a week or in the freezer for up to six months.

MEAT DISHES

BOEREWORS BRAII

Spicy sausage with tomato and mushroom sauce,
game chips andceleriac *rémoulade*
See photograph

Inspired by her South African husband, Sarah Raymond brought along some boerewors spicy sausages. She told us that since having baby Jessica, she's found herself at home spending hours in the kitchen experimenting and has entertained half of Hertfordshire! Ross came up with a new dish for her to impress her guests.

SERVES 2

FOR THE SAUSAGES
350 g (12 oz) boerewors (South African spicy beef sausage) or Cumberland sausage
2 tablespoons olive oil
1 onion, finely chopped
100 g (4 oz) button mushrooms
400 g (14 oz) can of chopped tomatoes
1 tablespoon balsamic vinegar
6 torn fresh basil leaves

FOR THE GAME CHIPS
1 medium-sized sweet potato
Oil, for deep-frying

FOR THE *RÉMOULADE* SALAD
1 egg yolk
1 teaspoon white-wine vinegar
1 teaspoon caster sugar
1 teaspoon Dijon mustard
150 ml (5 fl oz) olive oil
175 g (6 oz) celeriac, peeled and grated
2 tablespoons snipped fresh chives
Salt and freshly ground black pepper

Push two bamboo skewers, in a cross, through the sausage, to hold it in shape. Heat a tablespoon of oil in a griddle pan or frying-pan, add the sausage and cook for 10–15 minutes, turning occasionally, until it's cooked through.

Cook the onion in another tablespoon of oil for 3 minutes. Add the mushrooms and cook for 2 minutes. Stir in the tomatoes, and leave to simmer for 7–8 minutes. Add the vinegar and basil.

Heat the oil for deep-frying to 190°C/375°F or until a cube of day-old bread browns in 30 seconds. Finely slice the sweet potato or cut it into lattice game chips with a mandolin. Deep-fry for 2–3 minutes, until golden and crisp. Drain on absorbent kitchen paper.

Whisk the egg yolk, vinegar, sugar and mustard and season. Whisk in the olive oil very slowly, to make a creamy mayonnaise. Toss the celeriac and chives into the mayonnaise, to make a *rémoulade* salad. Season with salt and pepper.

To serve, spoon the tomato and mushroom sauce on to a serving plate and place the sausage on top. Pile the game chips on top of the sausage. Serve the *rémoulade* salad in a separate bowl.

READY STEADY COOK Tip
Use a food processor to make the mayonnaise. This allows the oil to be added very slowly. If your mayonnaise curdles, start again with 1 egg yolk and add the curdled mixture very, very slowly.

ROSS BURDEN

DOWN-HOME CHOW

Spare ribs with sweetcorn fritters and home-baked beans

Karen Marshall instantly impressed our audience when she told Fern she used to be housekeeper for Wonderwoman (Linda Carter). Karen is, however, very accident-prone and whilst there managed to back Linda's car into a mirror and nearly set her house on fire!

SERVES 2	1 large sprig of fresh rosemary, leaves chopped
FOR THE SPARE RIBS	Tabasco sauce
2 oranges	750 g (1½ lb) pork spare ribs, halved
2 tablespoons clear honey	50 g (2 oz) dried apricots
1 tablespoon balsamic vinegar	Salt and freshly ground black pepper

FOR THE BAKED BEANS
1 red pepper, seeded and sliced into strips
2 tablespoons olive oil
4 tomatoes, chopped
400 g (14 oz) can of soya beans, drained
2 tablespoons tomato purée
1 tablespoon black treacle
Tabasco sauce
Salt and freshly ground black pepper

FOR THE SWEETCORN FRITTERS
1 egg
25 g (1 oz) caster sugar
100 g (4 oz) self-raising flour
100 ml (4 fl oz) milk
50 g (2 oz) shelled pecan nuts, chopped
200 g (7 oz) can of sweetcorn kernels, drained
Salt and freshly ground black pepper
Sprigs of fresh flatleaf parsley and lemon wedges, to garnish

Remove strips of zest from the oranges and put them in a bowl. Squeeze the juice from the oranges and add to the zest, with the honey, the vinegar, rosemary and a few drops of Tabasco sauce; season to taste. Mix well, add the spare ribs and stir to coat the ribs in the marinade. If you have time, leave to marinate in the fridge overnight.

Take the ribs out of the marinade and cook in a moderately hot griddle pan or on a barbecue for 15–20 minutes (25 minutes if you prefer your ribs well-done), turning and brushing with the marinade from time to time.

Meanwhile, put the dried apricots in a bowl, cover with boiling water and set aside to soak.

Cook the red pepper in the olive oil for 2 minutes. Add the tomatoes and seasoning and cook for 2 minutes. Stir in the soya beans, tomato purée, treacle, a few drops of Tabasco sauce and 4 tablespoons of water and leave to simmer for 10–12 minutes, until thickened.

Whisk the egg and sugar and then whisk in the flour and milk, to make a smooth batter. Stir in the pecan nuts and the sweetcorn and season. Heat a lightly oiled griddle or heavy-based frying-pan. Spoon 5 tablespoons of the mixture into the frying-pan or griddle in heaps and flatten slightly. Cook for 5–6 minutes, turning once, until golden.

Drain the dried apricots and scatter them into the griddle pan, with the ribs, and cook for 3 minutes. To serve, spoon the baked beans into a serving bowl and serve with the ribs and sweetcorn fritters. Garnish with flatleaf parsley and lemon wedges.

ROSS BURDEN

KAYLET'S CUTLETS

Lamb filo parcels, tomato sauce and pickled carrot ribbons

'I'm on my second husband,' Kay Penfold told Fern. 'The first hated my cooking, so I need some serious tips to help keep this one!' Ross came to the rescue with this stylish lamb dish.

SERVES 2

FOR THE FILO PARCELS
4 lamb chops, trimmed
4 sheets of filo pastry, cut into 15 cm (6 inch) squares
50 g (2 oz) butter, melted
8 fresh mint leaves

FOR THE TOMATO SAUCE
2 tablespoons olive oil
1 onion, finely chopped
5 tomatoes, roughly chopped
2 tablespoons chopped fresh parsley
Salt and freshly ground black pepper

FOR THE CARROT PICKLE
200 ml (7 fl oz) white-wine vinegar
2 tablespoons caster sugar
1 garlic clove, crushed
6 cloves
4 carrots, sliced into thin ribbons, using a potato peeler
1 tablespoon poppy seeds
Salt and freshly ground black pepper

Pre-heat the oven to gas mark 6, 200°C, 400°F. Heat a char-grill or a frying-pan until very hot. Season the chops and brown on both sides; remove from the heat.

Brush each sheet of filo with melted butter. Place a chop on each filo sheet and add two mint leaves. Wrap the filo around the chop, leaving the bone poking out. Glaze the filo parcels with melted butter. Bake for 10–15 minutes.

Heat the olive oil and fry the onion until soft and translucent.

Add the tomatoes and chopped parsley then season and cook for 8–10 minutes, stirring occasionally, until thickened.

Put the vinegar, sugar, garlic and cloves into a pan and season with salt and pepper. Bring to the boil and leave to simmer until the sugar has completely dissolved. Put the carrot ribbons in a bowl and pour over the spiced vinegar; weigh it down, using a smaller bowl of water as a weight. Leave to pickle for 5 minutes.

To serve, place the chops on a plate and accompany with the tomato sauce. Garnish with the drained carrots, sprinkled with poppy seeds.

R O S S B U R D E N

PORK DIANE

Pork with celery in cream and mustard sauce, potato galettes, caramelized onions and tomato salad
See photograph

Jazz-lover Diane Thomas decided to bring pork along for Ross, as she'd recently had disasters with lamb and chicken. She'd cooked a chicken leaving a washer inside and a joint of lamb, only to find the next-door dog licking it.

SERVES 2
300 g (10½ oz) whole pork fillet, trimmed

FOR THE CELERY
2 trimmed celery hearts
440 ml (15 fl oz) can of dry cider
150 ml (5 fl oz) double cream
2 teaspoons wholegrain mustard
Salt and freshly ground black pepper

FOR THE ONION MARMALADE
2 tablespoons sunflower oil
1 large onion, thinly sliced
1 tablespoon sugar
2 tablespoons balsamic vinegar

FOR THE POTATO GALETTES
1 large potato, peeled
1 tablespoon sunflower oil
15 g (½ oz) butter

FOR THE TOMATO SALAD
4 tomatoes, skinned, seeded and chopped
2 tablespoons olive oil
6–10 large fresh basil leaves
Salt and freshly ground black pepper
Sprigs of fresh flatleaf parsley, to garnish

Place the celery hearts in a microwavable dish and pour over the cider. Cover with cling film and pierce. Microwave on full power for 10 minutes, or until tender.

To make the onion marmalade, heat the oil in a medium-size pan and sauté the onion. When softened, add the sugar and continue cooking over low heat for 8–10 minutes, to caramelize. Add the vinegar and 2 tablespoons of water, just before serving.

Sear the whole pork fillet in a non-stick pan, to brown it lightly on all sides. Then cook under a medium grill for about 10–15 minutes, turning occasionally, until cooked through and no longer pink in the centre.

Slice the potato fairly thinly with a sharp knife or mandolin. Overlap slices to make two circular cakes 8–10 cm (3–4 inches) across. Heat the oil and butter together in a large frying-pan. With a fish slice, carefully lift the potato galettes into the pan and cook for 4 minutes on both sides, until golden brown.

Put the tomatoes into a small bowl, add the olive oil and season with salt and pepper. Make a pile of 6–10 large basil leaves, roll up tightly and shred them finely. Sprinkle over the tomatoes.

Drain the cider from the celery into a pan and boil it fast over a high heat, to reduce to about 5 tablespoons. Add the cream and mustard and season to taste.

To serve, carve the pork fillet diagonally into thick slices and place on serving plates. Spoon the onion marmalade next to it.

Serve the celery with the cider sauce poured over and then place the potato galettes on the plates, topped with a little tomato relish. Garnish with a little flatleaf parsley.

READY STEADY COOK Tip
You may need to grill the pork fillet for longer, depending on its size and thickness. Take care not to overcook it, though, or it will end up tough!

MEAT DISHES

ROSS BURDEN

STEAK SAVOY

Steaks with cream sauce, stuffed cabbage-leaf rolls and potato röstis

Pat Dolan confessed that she married her husband Jack because he looked a bit like Barry Manilow – her great love in life. 'He's got the same long legs and droopy eyes,' she said. Ross cooked up this special steak for Pat and Jack.

SERVES 2

FOR THE STUFFED CABBAGE LEAVES
4 Savoy cabbage leaves (choose nice-looking, same-sized leaves)
4 mushrooms, finely chopped
7 baby Italian onions or 1 large onion, finely chopped
3 garlic cloves, crushed
25 g (1 oz) butter
Freshly ground black pepper
1 tablespoon chopped fresh rosemary
1 egg, beaten

FOR THE RÖSTIS
2 medium potatoes, grated

50 g (2 oz) butter
Salt and freshly ground black pepper

FOR THE STEAKS
2 fillet steaks
1 tablespoon olive oil
9 tablespoons white wine
4 tablespoons double cream
25 g (1 oz) butter
Salt and freshly ground black pepper

TO GARNISH
1 tomato, skinned, seeded and very finely chopped
10 fresh tarragon leaves, chopped

Remove the spines of the cabbage leaves and blanch them for 1–2 minutes, until they are soft. Refresh the leaves under cold water.

Sauté the mushrooms, six onions (or ¾ of 1 large onion) and two cloves of garlic in the butter, until soft. Season with pepper and chopped rosemary. Transfer this mixture to a bowl and stir in the egg. Put 1–2 spoonfuls of the mixture into each cabbage leaf, roll up the cabbage leaves to make parcels and steam them for 5 minutes. Put them seam-side down to cook.

For the röstis, squeeze all the water out of the grated potato, and season. Then heat the butter in a frying-pan. Place a metal ring in the pan and spoon the seasoned, grated potato into the ring. Press down, cook for 2 minutes, and then remove the ring and continue to cook until the potato is golden brown on both sides. Repeat to make a second rösti.

Season the steaks and cook on a griddle, for 4–5 minutes on each side.

To make the sauce, cook the remaining onion and garlic in a tablespoon of olive oil for 3–4 minutes, stirring occasionally, until they are soft. Add the wine and cook for 8 minutes. Stir in the cream and whisk in the butter. Continue to cook for a further 3–4 minutes. Strain the sauce through a fine sieve.

To serve, place the potato rösti on top of the steak and the stuffed cabbage leaves to the side. Surround with the sauce. Garnish with the tomato and chopped tarragon.

ROSS BURDEN

EAST-WEST LAMB

Lamb chops with aubergine fritters, roasted tomatoes and marrow chutney

Johanna came on the show and challenged her mother-in-law, Rita, by daring to claim she was the better cook. Husband Simon just watched nervously from the audience. Ross cooked up this delicious spicy lamb dish, to prove he was the greatest cook of them all!

SERVES 2

FOR THE LAMB CHOPS
2 x 175 g (6 oz) lamb steaks
3 tablespoons olive oil
2 tablespoons chopped fresh rosemary

FOR THE ROAST TOMATOES
4 tomatoes, sliced

2 tablespoons olive oil
2 garlic cloves, crushed
Salt and freshly ground black pepper

FOR THE MARROW CHUTNEY
1 onion, chopped
225 g (8 oz) marrow, peeled, seeded and roughly chopped

MEAT DISHES

50 g (2 oz) soft light brown sugar
50 g (2 oz) currants
2 tablespoons white-wine vinegar
1 teaspoon ground cumin
½ teaspoon ground turmeric
Salt and freshly ground black pepper

FOR THE AUBERGINE FRITTERS
1 small aubergine, cut in 1 cm (½ inch) slices
100 g (4 oz) couscous
Grated zest of 1 orange
1 tablespoon chopped fresh sage
Plain flour for coating
2 eggs, beaten
2 tablespoons olive oil
Salt
Sprigs of fresh rosemary, to garnish

Pre-heat the oven to gas mark 6, 200°C, 400°F. Put the slices of aubergine in a colander, sprinkle generously with salt and leave to drain.

Put the lamb, olive oil and rosemary in a bowl. Stir to coat well and set aside to marinate.

Arrange the tomato slices, overlapping slightly, in an ovenproof dish. Drizzle over 2 tablespoons of olive oil and sprinkle over the crushed garlic and salt and pepper. Roast for 10 minutes.

Put the onion, marrow, sugar, currants, vinegar, cumin, turmeric and salt and pepper in a pan. Simmer for 15 minutes, stirring occasionally.

Cook the lamb steaks with a little of the marinade in a frying-pan for 6 minutes, turning once.

Mix the couscous, orange zest and chopped sage. Rinse the aubergine slices and then dip them in the flour, then the beaten eggs and coat with the couscous mixture. Heat 2 tablespoons of oil in a large frying-pan, add the aubergine slices in batches and fry for 4 minutes, turning once, until golden brown. Drain on kitchen paper.

To serve, arrange the lamb steaks on serving plates, with the couscous-coated aubergine, and garnish with sprigs of rosemary.

Serve the roasted tomatoes and marrow chutney separately.

APPLE-BLACK POTATO STACK WITH HONEY-GLAZED PARSNIPS

Stacks of baked apple rings, sautéd potatoes, black pudding and deep-fried onion rings

Anne Ritson from Tyne and Wear told Ainsley that she wished he could be in her kitchen all the time. At home, her husband Alan 'is just constantly in the way'.

SERVES 2

FOR THE APPLE RINGS

2 dessert apples, peeled, cored and sliced in rings
2 teaspoons soft light brown sugar
½ teaspoon ground cinnamon

FOR THE PARSNIPS

2½ tablespoons olive oil
225 g (8 oz) baby parsnips
2 teaspoons clear honey
Juice of ½ lemon
Salt and freshly ground black pepper

FOR THE POTATO, ONION AND BLACK PUDDING

225 g (8 oz) potatoes, cut in 1 cm (½ inch) slices
1 onion, sliced
75 ml (3 fl oz) milk
Oil, for deep-frying
2 tablespoons olive oil
15 g (½ oz) butter
4 tablespoons plain flour, seasoned
275 g (10 oz) black pudding, cut in 2 cm (¾ inch) slices
Salt and freshly ground black pepper
Flatleaf parsley, to garnish

Pre-heat the oven to gas mark 7, 220°C, 425°F. Spread the apple rings on a greased baking tray, sprinkle over the sugar and cinnamon and put under a moderately hot grill for 10–15 minutes, turning once, until golden.

Heat the olive oil in a pan, add the parsnips and cook for 2 minutes. Add the honey and lemon juice and season with salt and pepper. Cover and cook for 3 minutes, turning occasionally. Transfer to a roasting tin and roast in the oven for 10–15 minutes, until crisp.

Cook the potatoes in a pan of boiling water for 4 minutes. Put the sliced onion in a bowl, with the milk, and leave for 5 minutes. Heat the oil for deep-frying to 190°C/375°F or until a cube of day-old bread browns in 30 seconds. Drain the potatoes well. Heat a tablespoon of olive oil and the butter in a frying-pan, add the potatoes, season and sauté for 8–10 minutes, turning once.

Drain the onion rings and coat with seasoned flour. Deep-fry for 2–3 minutes until golden and crisp. Drain on absorbent kitchen paper and keep hot.

Heat the last tablespoon of olive oil in a frying-pan, add the slices of black pudding and fry for 5–6 minutes, turning once.

To serve, layer up the apple rings, potatoes, black pudding and onion rings in the centre of two serving plates. Arrange the glazed parsnips around the edge and garnish with sprigs of flatleaf parsley.

AINSLEY HARRIOTT

BRYN'S 'AM AN' EGGS

Crisp-coated gammon steaks with poached eggs, with tomato sauce

Golf pro Bryn Morris admitted that he'll try anything once and the most unusual thing he'd eaten recently was pigeon. His favourite meal, however, is ham and eggs so he challenged Ainsley to make him a posh version.

SERVES 2	100 ml (3 fl oz) white wine
2 slices of dried bread (dry in the oven,	250 g (9 oz) cherry tomatoes, cut in half
if necessary)	1 tablespoon chopped fresh thyme
1 teaspoon dried mixed herbs	1 tablespoon tomato purée
6 tablespoons olive oil	100 g (4 oz) new potatoes, peeled into
1 onion, finely sliced	'barrel' shapes
1 yellow pepper	175 g (6 oz) sugar-snap peas
3 eggs	Juice of ½ lemon
2 x 200 g (7 oz) gammon steaks	½ tablespoon white-wine vinegar
75 g (3 oz) plain flour	Salt and freshly ground black pepper

Process the bread in a food processor to make breadcrumbs. Put into a glass bowl and add the dried herbs. In a frying-pan, heat 2 tablespoons of olive oil and fry the onion until it's almost caramelized. Blacken the skin of the pepper, by leaving it over a gas flame on the hob or by grilling it under a pre-heated grill for 10–15 minutes, turning occasionally. When completely blackened, put in a plastic bag until cool enough to handle. Take off the skin. Cut in half, seed and slice thinly.

Lightly beat one egg. Dip the gammon steaks into the flour, then the egg and finally the breadcrumbs. Shake off any excess. Leave to one side. When the onions are almost caramelized, add the wine, tomatoes, thyme and the tomato purée. Cook for 3 minutes. Season to taste.

Cook the potatoes and the sugar-snap peas in boiling, salted water. After 2 minutes, remove the sugar-snap peas, allowing the potatoes to continue cooking. Put the peas in a bowl and add a tablespoon of oil and the lemon juice. Season to taste.

Heat 2 tablespoons of olive oil in a frying-pan and fry the gammon steaks for about 5–6 minutes on each side. Bring a shallow pan of water to the boil, with the vinegar. Reduce the heat under the vinegar water and poach the eggs in it for 2–3 minutes, depending on personal preference. Drain the potatoes and toss in the last tablespoon of olive oil. Season to taste.

Garnish the plates with the sliced pepper and peas. Pour on the tomato mixture. Lay the gammon steaks on the plates, with the poached eggs on top. Serve with the potatoes.

READY STEADY COOK Tips

If you are substituting dried herbs for fresh herbs, remember that one teaspoon of dried herbs is equal to one tablespoon of chopped fresh herbs.

Place chopped herbs in small rigid containers, then pack in freezer-proof bags and use straight from the freezer.

FANCY FOOTBALL BIRYANI TEMPURA

Lamb biryani with tempura vegetables and piquant dipping sauce

Referee Eddie McGrath came on in his referee kit and lent his whistle to Fern so she could keep the chefs in tow. A bull once charged on to the pitch when he was refereeing a game. He said, 'The players in the red strip moved the quickest!'

SERVES 4

FOR THE SAUCE
1 orange
2 tablespoons tomato ketchup
1 tablespoon Worcestershire sauce
2 tablespoons honey
Cayenne pepper

FOR THE BIRYANI
3 lamb loin chops or boneless lamb, approximately 300 g (11 oz), cut into 2.5 cm (1 inch) cubes
1 teaspoon ground turmeric
1 teaspoon medium-hot curry powder
1 teaspoon ground cinnamon
1 tablespoon olive oil
1 garlic clove, finely chopped
3 tablespoons finely chopped fresh coriander
1 tablespoon vegetable oil

25 g (1 oz) butter
1 onion
1 red pepper, seeded
1 green pepper, seeded
1 lamb stock cube
200 g (7 oz) long-grain rice
Cayenne pepper
1 tablespoon chopped fresh flatleaf parsley
Salt and freshly ground black pepper

FOR THE TEMPURA
Vegetable oil, for deep-frying
2 egg whites
50 g (2 oz) cornflour
75 g (3 oz) plain flour
120 g (4½ oz) oyster mushrooms
Salt and freshly ground black pepper
1 lemon, cut into wedges, to serve

Grate the zest from the orange and squeeze the juice. Place in a small pan, with the tomato ketchup, Worcestershire sauce, honey and a pinch of cayenne pepper and leave to simmer gently for 10 minutes.

Meanwhile, for the biryani, place the lamb in a bowl and add the turmeric, curry powder, cinnamon, olive oil, garlic and 1 tablespoon of chopped fresh coriander, stirring to coat the lamb. Heat the vegetable oil, with the butter, in a large frying-pan, and sauté the lamb for 5 minutes. Thinly slice half the onion and half the red and green peppers and add to the pan, with the lamb stock cube. Stir to coat the vegetables and add 300 ml (10 fl oz) of hot water, the rice, a pinch of cayenne pepper, 1 tablespoon of fresh coriander and the parsley. Season well. Cover the pan and leave to simmer for 15 minutes, until the liquid is absorbed and the rice is tender, adding more hot water as required.

Meanwhile, for the tempura heat oil for deep-frying, until almost smoking. Place the egg whites in a bowl and add the cornflour, plain flour and enough water to make a thick batter (about 85 ml (3 fl oz)). Whisk for 2 minutes and then season. Thickly slice the other half of the onion, red and green peppers, leaving a few thin slices for decoration. Wipe the mushrooms. Dip the vegetables in the batter in batches and deep-fry at 190°C/375°F for 2–3 minutes, until the batter is golden. Drain on kitchen paper.

To serve, decorate a large plate with the reserved thin slices of vegetables. Place the rice and lamb mixture in the middle of the plate and surround with the deep-fried vegetables. Sprinkle over the remaining chopped coriander and place the lemon wedges to one side. Pour the sauce into a small bowl and serve as a dipping sauce.

READY STEADY COOK Tip
You could use 300 g (11 oz) of boneless lamb, cut into 2.5 cm (1 inch) cubes, instead of loin chops.

AINSLEY HARRIOTT

LISA'S LAZY LAMB AND LENTIL CURRY

Lamb, lentil and aubergine curry, with little naan breads
and onion wedges
See photograph

Lisa Balbes wanted Ainsley to create something special for her fiancé Paul, who was literally the
boy next door. 'It comes in very handy if we have a row,' she explained,
'as I don't have far to stomp home!'

SERVES 4

FOR THE CURRY

200 g (7 oz) boneless lamb leg steak, cubed
2 limes
2 teaspoons curry powder
Cayenne pepper
120 g (4½ oz) red lentils, rinsed
2 tablespoons vegetable oil
2 garlic cloves, crushed
5 cloves
4 cardamom pods
2 potatoes, peeled and cut into 1 cm (½ inch) cubes
1 onion, finely chopped

1 vegetable stock cube
1 tablespoon tomato purée
3 tablespoons chopped fresh coriander
3 tablespoons olive oil
1 aubergine, cut into 2.5 cm (1 inch) cubes
6 tablespoons crème fraiche

FOR THE NAAN BREADS

6 tablespoons plain flour
6 tablespoons vegetable oil
2 tablespoons chopped fresh coriander
1 tablespoon tomato purée
1 onion, cut into 6, lengthways, with skin left on

Place the lamb in a bowl, with the juice from 1 lime, the curry powder
and a pinch of cayenne pepper. Leave to one side, to marinate for
5 minutes.

Cook the lentils in boiling water until softened, for about 10 minutes.
Meanwhile, heat the vegetable oil in a large pan. Add the garlic,
cloves and cardamom pods and the lamb. Stir-fry over a medium heat

for 5 minutes. Add the potato and onion. Drain the lentils and add to the pan, with the stock cube, tomato purée, 2 tablespoons of chopped coriander and 175 ml (6 fl oz) boiling water, to make a curry consistency. Simmer for 5 minutes.

Heat the olive oil in a frying-pan over a medium heat and add the aubergine cubes. Sauté for 10 minutes, until cooked, stirring occasionally.

For the naan breads, mix the flour and 2 tablespoons of vegetable oil with the chopped coriander, tomato purée and enough water to make a soft dough. Divide the mixture into four and pat each quarter with your hands to make four flat, round patties. Brush the patties and onion wedges with the remaining 4 tablespoons of vegetable oil. Heat a frying-pan over a high heat and place the patties and onion wedges in the dry pan. Fry for 2–3 minutes on either side, until golden.

Add the cooked aubergine to the lamb and lentils, with 4 tablespoons of the crème fraiche and the juice from the second lime. Add a little more water, if it looks too dry. Stir well and heat through.

To serve, place the curry on a large plate and surround with the little naan breads. Pour over the last 2 tablespoons of crème fraiche and garnish with the onion wedges. Sprinkle over a small pinch of cayenne pepper and the remaining chopped coriander.

READY STEADY COOK Tips
To save time, you could use canned lentils, which are already cooked, instead of dried lentils. As a general rule, pulses such as lentils and chick peas double their weight when cooked, so if the recipe calls for 120 g (4½ oz) red lentils, you'll need a 250 g (9 oz) can.

FLAMBOYANT FLASH-FLAMING STEAK WITH JAZZY POTATOES

Steaks with green peppercorn and cream sauce,
fried potatoes and orange salad

Trainee nurse Vicky Gambleton chopped very carefully. 'I may be a nurse, but I'm a bit squeamish — I fainted at my first operation!' Ainsley thought she did very well indeed.

SERVES 2
FOR THE STEAKS
450 g (1 lb) new potatoes, scrubbed
1 garlic clove, chopped
2 sprigs of fresh rosemary
3 tablespoons olive oil
15 g (½ oz) butter
2 flash-fry steaks
Salt and freshly ground black pepper

FOR THE SAUCE
2 tablespoons green peppercorns in brine
2 shallots, finely chopped
2 tablespoons white wine
75 ml (3 fl oz) double cream

FOR THE SALAD
½ curly-leaved lettuce
2 oranges, segmented
Juice of ½ orange
½ teaspoon Dijon mustard
1 tablespoon chopped fresh coriander
2 tablespoons olive oil
Salt and freshly ground black pepper

Par-boil the potatoes for 8–10 minutes, until tender. Drain and slice the potatoes fairly thickly and fry them, with the garlic and rosemary, in 2 tablespoons of olive oil and 15 g (½ oz) of butter for 3–4 minutes, until golden brown.

Season the steaks and fry them in a tablespoon of olive oil, for 2–3 minutes on each side. Remove from the pan and keep warm.

For the pepper sauce, using the pan in which the steaks were cooked, fry the green peppercorns and shallots and 1 tablespoon of the juice from the green peppercorns. Add the white wine and cream and cook gently for 2 minutes.

Mix together the lettuce and oranges and arrange in a salad bowl. For the salad dressing, whisk together the orange juice, mustard, coriander and 2 tablespoons of olive oil. Season to taste.

To serve, arrange the steaks on a plate. Surround with the potatoes and pour over the sauce. Serve the salad separately.

AINSLEY HARRIOTT

THE CAJUN GLOUCESTERSHIRE OLD SPOT CHOP

Pork chop with griddled potato wedges,
vegetable fritters and rocket salad
See photograph

'I've brought you some local Gloucestershire Old Spot,' John Parker told Ainsley. 'But I'm a bit worried about being your contestant as, despite being told I'm the world's greatest cook, it was my dog who said it.' Ainsley's dog, Oscar, often tells him the same thing.

SERVES 2

FOR THE CHOP

2 medium-sized potatoes, cut into wedges
2 teaspoons black peppercorns
1 teaspoon ground cumin
1 teaspoon ground ginger
½ teaspoon chilli powder
½ teaspoon paprika
Grated zest of ½ and juice of 1 lime

1 tablespoon olive oil
1 x 750 g (1½ lb) Gloucestershire Old Spot pork chop

FOR THE FRITTERS

150 g (5 oz) runner beans, sliced diagonally
1 large red onion, cut into rings
4 tablespoons milk
2 teaspoons ground cinnamon

MEAT DISHES

300 ml (10 fl oz) vegetable oil	Salt
75 g (3 oz) plain flour	1 bunch of rocket, to serve
1 teaspoon ground allspice	1 tablespoon olive oil
1 teaspoon ground ginger	½ teaspoon paprika

Bring a pan of water to the boil and cook the potato wedges for
10 minutes, until soft. Drain and keep to one side. Meanwhile, put the
runner beans and onion rings for the fritters to soak in the milk, add a
teaspoon each of cinnamon and salt and keep to one side.

To make the marinade for the pork, crush the peppercorns in a pestle
and mortar. Mix in the cumin, 1 teaspoon of ginger, the chilli powder
and paprika. Then add the lime zest, half the lime juice and the oil and
mix to form a paste. Trim the fat off the pork and remove the bone. Make
a few slashes on each side, brush the marinade on both sides and leave
to one side while you pre-heat a griddle or non-stick frying-pan. Fry the
pork for 5–8 minutes each side. During the last 5 minutes of cooking, fry
the potato wedges, turning occasionally, until golden on all sides.

Heat the vegetable oil in a pan. In a bowl, mix together the flour,
allspice and remaining teaspoon of cinnamon and season with salt.
Drain the onions and beans and dip them in the seasoned flour. Fry in
the pan until golden. Drain on kitchen paper and sprinkle over the
teaspoon of ground ginger.

Arrange the rocket on a plate. Dress with a tablespoon of olive oil,
the remaining lime juice and ½ teaspoon of paprika. Put the deep-fried
vegetables in the centre of the plate. Place the pork on top. Arrange
the potato wedges around the plate.

READY STEADY COOK Tips
*If you can't find a Gloucestershire Old Spot chop, use 2 x 275 g
(10 oz) pork chops.*

*You could deep-fry the onions and beans in a deep-fat fryer at
190°C/375°F for 1–2 minutes until light, crisp and golden.*

DESSERTS

BUMPY'S BRÛLÉE

Cricket fan Hazel Southgate is known as Bumpy to her mates – it stems from being called Bumpkin as a child. Ross created this delicious brûlée for her to delight all her friends with.

SERVES 4–6

300 ml (10 fl oz) white wine
2 tablespoons caster sugar
6 dessert pears
225 g (8 oz) frozen raspberries, thawed
2 eggs
50 g (2 oz) blanched almonds, finely chopped

50 g (2 oz) self-raising flour
25 g (1 oz) butter
200 g (7 oz) Greek yoghurt
1 tablespoon light muscovado sugar
Fresh basil leaves, shredded
Salt

Put 150 ml (5 fl oz) of water, the wine and 1 tablespoon of caster sugar in a pan and heat gently. Peel and core four pears, add to the pan and poach for 10 minutes.

Put half the raspberries in a pan with the other tablespoon of caster sugar and cook for 3 minutes. Push through a sieve to make a sauce.

Beat the eggs and a pinch of salt together. Mix the almonds and flour in another bowl. Peel and core the two remaining pears and then slice into 1 cm (½ inch) thick rings. Dip in the beaten eggs and coat with the almond mixture. Melt the butter in a frying-pan, add the almond-coated pear rings and cook for 6–8 minutes, turning once, until golden and crisp. Pre-heat the grill to hot.

Lift the poached pears out of the wine, with a slotted spoon. Slice through the pears at 1 cm (½ inch) intervals, leaving the stalk end intact. Fan out the pears and put them in a flameproof dish. Scatter over the rest of the raspberries and spoon over the Greek yoghurt. Sprinkle the brown sugar over the top. Grill for 4 minutes, until the sugar has caramelized (or use a blow torch!).

Pour the raspberry sauce over the pear fritters and sprinkle the shredded basil over the top. Serve with the caramelized poached pears.

SKIP'S GLOOP

The very brave Mat Beardall came on the show to challenge his mother-in-law, Barbara. Both Mat and Barbara are Scout leaders and came on in full uniform to challenge the chefs to make a couple of delicious meals that they could teach the troops! Ross's marshmallow treat will certainly become a campfire favourite.

SERVES 6	
200 g (7 oz) granulated sugar	2 bananas, thinly sliced
300 ml (10 fl oz) double cream	2 eating apples, cored and sliced
200 g (7 oz) marshmallows	225 g (8 oz) plain chocolate
1 medium-sized Swiss roll	25 g (1 oz) butter
Vanilla essence	Icing sugar, to dust
	Sprigs of fresh mint, to decorate

Put the granulated sugar in a heavy-based pan and just cover with water. Heat gently, until the sugar has dissolved. Boil steadily, without stirring, for 8–10 minutes, until the syrup turns to caramel and is golden brown.

Pour all but 2 tablespoons of the cream into a pan and heat gently. Add all but six of the marshmallows and stir until melted and smooth. Carefully unroll the Swiss roll on a large piece of foil. Sprinkle over a few drops of vanilla essence and a tablespoon of the caramel. Spread half the cream and marshmallow mixture over the Swiss roll and arrange the slices of banana on top. Starting from one long side, roll up the Swiss roll, lifting the foil to help. Wrap the Swiss roll in the foil and chill in the fridge for at least 10 minutes.

Stir the rest of the cream and marshmallow mixture into the caramel. Add the apple slices and simmer for 5 minutes.

Break the chocolate into a pan, add 225 ml (8 fl oz) of water and heat gently, until melted and smooth. Whisk in the reserved 2 tablespoons of double cream and the butter, until melted.

To serve, put the Swiss roll on a deep serving plate and dust with icing sugar. Spoon the apples and caramel-marshmallow sauce on each side. Scatter over the remaining marshmallows and pour the chocolate sauce over the top. Decorate with sprigs of mint.

R O S S   B U R D E N

MY KNEES CRUMBLE

Rhubarb and ginger crumble, with honey and vanilla custard
See photograph

A well-seasoned traveller, Alison Millward told us that the most unusual thing she'd ever eaten was in Peru and that was fried guinea pig! Ross's dessert is slightly more traditional and far more tasty, we think.

SERVES 3
FOR THE CRUMBLE
175 g (6 oz) caster sugar
450 g (1 lb) bundle of rhubarb (about 6 large stalks), cut into 5 mm (¼ inch) chunks
5 whole stem ginger, in syrup, drained and chopped
175 g (6 oz) plain flour
75 g (3 oz) butter
50 g (2 oz) ground almonds

FOR THE CUSTARD
5 medium egg yolks (size 3)
1 tablespoon honey
300 ml (10 fl oz) double cream
50 g (2 oz) caster sugar
1 vanilla pod or 1 teaspoon vanilla essence
75 ml (3 fl oz) milk

Pre-heat the oven to gas mark 6, 200°C, 400°F. Put 300 ml (10 fl oz) of water in a pan, add 75 g (3 oz) of caster sugar and bring to the boil. Turn down the heat and poach the rhubarb in the syrup for 4 minutes, until softened. Drain and return to the pan, reserving the syrup. Mix in the ginger and put into an ovenproof dish. Add 2 tablespoons of the syrup.

Rub the flour and butter together in a mixing bowl. Add the almonds and 75 g (3 oz) of the sugar and mix thoroughly, until the mixture resembles breadcrumbs. Spoon the crumble mixture on top of the rhubarb and ginger and bake for 15–20 minutes.

Meanwhile, to make the custard, whisk the egg yolks and honey together, until the mixture turns a pale yellow colour.

Heat the cream and 50 g (2 oz) of caster sugar slowly in a pan. Add the vanilla pod or vanilla essence and milk. When the mixture is nearly boiling, remove from the heat and pour into the egg yolks and honey mixture, whisking vigorously. Return to the heat, stirring constantly, and cook until the custard has thickened enough to coat the back of a wooden spoon. This takes about 20 minutes.

Serve the rhubarb and ginger crumble with the honey and vanilla custard.

READY STEADY COOK Tip
Don't let the custard boil, or it will curdle.

R O S S   B U R D E N

TARTE TRACIAN

Tracy Dalglish loves puds, but wasn't so hot at making them and asked Ross if he could show her a quick, cheap yet sumptuous dessert to impress her mates at dinner parties. Ross obliged with this lovely fruit tart.

SERVES 2

225 g (8 oz) puff pastry
5 tablespoons caster sugar
75 g (3 oz) butter

3 Cox's apples, peeled, cored and cut into eighths
450 g (1 lb) frozen summer fruit mix, thawed
3 egg yolks
300 ml (10 fl oz) milk

Pre-heat the oven to gas mark 9, 240°C, 475°F. Roll out the pastry to make a thin, 18 cm (7 inch) circle. Let the pastry rest in the refrigerator for 10 minutes (or overnight if possible).

Melt 3 tablespoons of the sugar and the butter until the sugar dissolves. Add the apple slices and cook until the mixture thickens and turns golden brown and sticky. Arrange the caramelized apples in an 18 cm (7 inch) round, ovenproof dish and spoon over any extra juice. Lay the pastry over the apples and trim so the pastry fits the dish. Bake for 7–10 minutes, until the pastry has puffed up and turned golden brown.

To make the fruit custard, pass the summer fruits through a sieve, to make a purée. Whisk together the egg yolks and remaining sugar in a bowl. Stir in half of the fruit purée.

Meanwhile, heat the milk almost to boiling point. Pour the hot milk into the egg mixture, stirring continually. Then pour the mixture back into the saucepan and heat very gently until the custard has thickened, whisking all the time. Do not let the custard boil or it will curdle.

To serve, turn the tart out on to a plate; the pastry should be on the bottom. Serve with the fruit custard and remaining fruit purée.

READY STEADY COOK Tips

Use a dish without handles as it will make the tarte easier to turn out.

Don't be tempted to stir the apples while they are in the pan or they will start to break up and not look so attractive when the tart is served. Simply leave them gently bubbling in the sugar and butter until slightly softened and golden.

A I N S L E Y   H A R R I O T T

TRIPLE CHOC NUT AND APPLE PANCAKES

Chocolate and apple pancakes, with red wine, curd and cardamom pears

Rosalind McPartlin told us how she had to go ex-directory because she has the same surname as Ant in 'Ant and Dec' and they kept getting phone calls from screaming teenage girls!

SERVES 4

FOR THE PEARS
25 g (1 oz) soft light brown sugar
300 ml (10 fl oz) red wine
6 cardamom pods
2 firm dessert pears, peeled and halved
100 g (4 oz) curd cheese

FOR THE CHOCOLATE NUTS
175 g (6 oz) plain chocolate, broken into pieces
75 g (3 oz) walnut halves

FOR THE PANCAKE BATTER
300 ml (10 fl oz) milk
1 egg
100 g (4 oz) plain flour
Salt
2 tablespoons chocolate icing sugar

FOR THE PANCAKE FILLING
1 orange
25 g (1 oz) butter
1 large cooking apple, peeled, cored and cut in 1 cm (½ in) chunks
2 tablespoons white wine
2 tablespoons caster sugar

TO DECORATE
Icing sugar
Sprigs of fresh mint

For the pears, put the brown sugar, red wine and cardamom pods in a pan. Hollow out the pears slightly with a teaspoon and add the pear halves to the pan. Bring to the boil, reduce the heat and simmer for 15 minutes.

Meanwhile, for the nuts, put the chocolate in a heatproof bowl, place over a pan of hot (not boiling) water and leave until melted. Dip 50 g (2 oz) of the walnuts into the chocolate and put on a plate. Chill in the fridge, to set. Leave the rest of the melted chocolate over the pan of hot water.

For the pancakes, whisk the milk and the egg together. Sift the flour, a pinch of salt and the chocolate icing sugar into a bowl. Gradually beat in the milk and egg, to form a smooth batter.

For the filling, roughly chop the rest of the walnuts and cut a few needleshreds of zest from the orange, using a zester. Melt the butter in a pan, add the apple, white wine, caster sugar, chopped walnuts and orange needleshreds and cook gently for 8 minutes.

Heat a lightly oiled 20 cm (8 inch) frying-pan, add 5 tablespoons of the pancake batter and tilt to coat the base of the pan. Cook for 3–4 minutes, turning once. Repeat to make four pancakes. Keep the pancakes warm. Transfer the apple mixture to a bowl and stir in half of the melted chocolate. Spoon along the centre of the pancakes and roll up.

Slice the orange and cut one slice into quarters. Put the pancakes on a serving plate and scatter over the chocolate-coated nuts. Decorate with twisted slices of orange, drizzle over the rest of the melted chocolate and dust with icing sugar. Put the pears and cooking juices in a serving bowl. Spoon the curd cheese into the pears and decorate with the orange quarters and sprigs of mint.

READY STEADY COOK Tip
If you can't buy the chocolate-flavoured icing sugar, use 2 tablespoons of icing sugar and 1 teaspoon of cocoa powder, instead.

DEEP DEVON SUMMER-FRUIT SOUFFLÉ

Fruit soufflé with orange baskets and clotted cream

Janet Till treated all the camera crew by bringing them loads of clotted cream from her home in Newton Abbot, Devon. Not only was Janet able to tuck into an amazing summer pud from Ainsley, but she was seen from every best angle!

SERVES 2

2 medium oranges
3 eggs, separated
25 g (1 oz) plus 1 tablespoon caster sugar
15 g (½ oz) butter
150 ml (5 fl oz) white wine
225 g (8 oz) summer fruits, e.g. strawberries, raspberries and redcurrants, thawed if frozen

1 lime
4 tablespoons clotted cream
4 tablespoons strawberry jam
Icing sugar, to dust
Sprigs of fresh mint, to decorate

Place the oranges on a board, with the stalk end of each orange facing upwards. Make a vertical cut on each side of the stalk, one-third of the way through the skin and flesh of the orange. Cut each orange horizontally, in a zig-zag style, and then remove the loose sections, to make a 'basket' with a 'handle'.

Scoop the orange flesh out of the baskets with a teaspoon. Remove the stalk from the handle of each basket and make a small hole in the top of the handle. Push a sprig of mint into the hole.

Put the egg yolks and a tablespoon of sugar in a bowl and whisk for 2 minutes, until pale and creamy. Whisk the egg whites to stiff peaks and then fold into the egg-yolk mixture. Melt the butter in a 23 cm (9 inch) frying-pan. Add the egg mixture and spread evenly over the base of the pan. Cook over a gentle heat for 4–5 minutes, until the underside is golden.

DESSERTS

Put the 25 g (1 oz) of sugar and the wine in a pan. Put the summer fruits in a colander over the pan and press down with a saucer to let the juice trickle into the pan. Squeeze in the juice from one of the unused sections of orange. Bring to the boil and simmer for about 3 minutes so that the liquid is reduced by half and becomes syrupy. Fold in the summer fruits and cook for 5 minutes. Cut the lime in half, in a zig-zag style, and scoop out the lime flesh. Pile the clotted cream into the lime shells. Fill the orange baskets with some of the hot summer fruits.

Put the soufflé omelette under a pre-heated grill for 3 minutes until the top is golden. Spread the jam over the omelette and spoon over the rest of the hot summer fruits. Fold the omelette in half and transfer to a serving plate. Dust with icing sugar and mark in a lattice pattern on the top with a hot skewer. Serve the soufflé omelette with the orange baskets and cream-filled lime shells, decorated with a sprig of mint.

AINSLEY HARRIOTT

ORANGE CHOCOLATE MOUNTAINS

Sweet-toothed Jackie Weaver came along with a bag of her favourite goodies for Ainsley to transform into this wonderful dessert.

SERVES 4

175 g (6 oz) plain chocolate	Zest of 2 oranges
5 amaretti biscuits	Juice of ½ lemon
5 tablespoons desiccated coconut	2 tablespoons chopped hazelnuts
600 ml (1 pint) double cream	100 g (4 oz) icing sugar
90 ml (3 fl oz) white wine	10 physalis (Cape gooseberries)
75 g (3 oz) caster sugar	3 blood oranges, peeled and sliced
	Sprigs of fresh mint, to garnish

Break the chocolate into pieces and melt in the microwave on a medium setting, for approximately 3 minutes. Check the chocolate after 2 minutes, to ensure that it does not overcook.

Dip three of the amaretti in the chocolate and then roll them in 3 tablespoons of the desiccated coconut. Set to one side, on baking parchment.

To make the chocolate truffle mousse, whip the cream to soft peaks and then fold in the remaining melted chocolate, with a metal spoon. Then fold in two crushed amaretti biscuits.

For the sauce, mix together the wine, sugar and orange zest and cook for 5 minutes. Stir in the lemon juice, hazelnuts and 2 tablespoons of coconut. Cook for a further 3–4 minutes, until thick and syrupy.

Mix the icing sugar with 3–4 tablespoons of water: the mixture should be of a fairly thick consistency. Dip the physalis into the icing sugar and stand on baking parchment to set.

To serve, arrange the orange slices in the base of a wide bowl. Pipe or spoon the chocolate truffle mousse over the oranges and in the centre. Spoon over the sauce and decorate the dish with the physalis and dipped amaretti biscuits. Garnish with fresh mint leaves.

READY STEADY COOK Tip
The mousse would benefit from being chilled for 2 hours before serving.

A I N S L E Y   H A R R I O T T

VICKY'S CHOCOLATE NUT CRUNCH

See photograph

Vicky Hext admitted to Ainsley that she is a very fussy eater and lives off breakfast cereal and chocolate — and she's getting a little bored with it, so she asked Ainsley to make it a bit more exciting.

SERVES 2	1 x 30 g (1 oz) variety pack of Crunchy
450 g (1 lb) strawberries	Nut Cornflakes
1 tablespoon white wine	150 ml (5 fl oz) double cream
100 g (4 oz) puff pastry	2 kiwi fruit, peeled and sliced
1 egg beaten with ½ tablespoon water	Icing sugar, for dusting
100 g (4 oz) cooking chocolate, at least	Zest and segments of an orange
70 % cocoa solids	

Pre-heat the oven to gas mark 7, 220°C, 425°F. Blend half the strawberries in a blender, with the wine, until smooth. Flour the work surface and roll out the pastry to about 2 mm (⅛ inch) thick. Prick all over with a fork. Using a small saucepan or a 20 cm (8 inch) plate as a template, cut out two discs. Put on two greased baking sheets. Brush both with the beaten egg and bake for 8–10 minutes, until well risen and golden brown.

Melt three-quarters of the chocolate in a double-boiler or bowl set over a saucepan of hot water. Hull and slice the remaining strawberries. Stir the cornflakes into the chocolate and then spread evenly on to baking parchment. Put on a plate and put in the fridge or freezer to cool for 20 minutes. Take the pastry out of the oven and flatten one disc.

Whip the double cream to soft peaks. Spread half the cream on the flattened pastry disc. Lay a third of the sliced strawberries on the cream, with a third of the kiwi slices. Take the chocolate crunch out of the fridge. Peel off the paper, break into pieces and arrange on top of the fruit. Spread the remaining cream on top and then add more kiwi and strawberries. Finally, put the other pastry disc on top. Grate the remaining chocolate over the plate, dust with icing sugar and scatter on the orange zest. Around the edge of the plate decorate with the orange segments and the remaining kiwi and strawberries. Serve the purée separately.

READY STEADY COOK Tips

If you don't already own a zester, make sure you invest in one now. They're cheap, and easy to clean, as well as being quick and efficient to use.

Non-stick baking paper, sometimes called parchment, is great for things containing a high proportion of sugar. But you can lightly grease, then use greaseproof paper if that is all you have. Gaining popularity are fabric reusable 'magic' papers. After use you simply wipe over and they are ready for use again. They also withstand domestic oven temperatures.

INDEX

I N D E X